Praise

My Darling fr

CW01551814

"I provide few endorsemer
my schedule does not allow for car___ ___ ___ading of manuscripts
and partly because I realize the power of endorsements. I was
invited to review the manuscript, *My Darling From the Lions*. The
first reading of this book was quite intriguing—a young son's
challenges became a family's journey. The second reading
revealed the depth of soul-searching experiences, divine guidance for a mother and father as they retrieved a son who had
been victimized by pornography, chat rooms, homosexuality, and
peer abuse."

"Daniel was a young man whose personal characteristics
made him vulnerable to peer abuse—he was sensitive, intelligent,
perfectionistic, all envied traits by his peers. Perhaps without
intention or motive, they pushed him to the outer edges of their
friendship, and in some ways drove him to pornography and
chat rooms as a way to deal with his depression. Little was
Daniel aware of the addictive qualities of such activities. But a
mother's and father's love for their son was more powerful than
the forces that tried to take him from them."

"The real hero in this story is not the mother, nor father,
nor the kind ecclesiastical leader. The real hero is Daniel whose
indomitable spirit allowed him to traverse some rough terrain,
and to become whole again. More importantly, those same characteristics that made Daniel vulnerable to challenges have now
become gifts of the spirit that will allow him to lift others—
because he has been there."

"The book provides hope for individuals and families—that
change is possible. I am pleased to provide my endorsement."

—Dr. A. Dean Byrd, Clinical Professor,
University of Utah School of Medicine.

"As I cried and rejoiced through this book, I saw a typical, by-the-numbers Mormon mother transform into one who had a deep relationship with the Savior. This book shows how miracles occur when we refuse to give up on ourselves or our children, and truly put our foundation in Christ."

"Anyone who professes to believe in the Atonement must accept this story or be guilty of hypocrisy. I believe sharing this sensitive experience is just what Christ would have this author do. The true principles contained in *My Darling From the Lions* encompass the most important lessons we can learn in this life. The fact that it is made up entirely of journal entries makes this book amazing and unique."

—Merrill Osmond, entertainer and inspirational author.

"Thank you for the opportunity of reviewing and commenting on [this] book written by a mother whose son got ensnared by pornography and homosexuality and eventually recovered from its influence. I have had experience . . . treating more than 400 clients (mostly LDS) over 15 years who have been addicted to pornography and a few with homosexual inclinations."

"I like the book. I like its honesty and spiritual core. I also find that a significant part of healing involves merciful blessings from heaven after we have done our part to repent and change our ways. Every mom who reads this will identify with many of the things [the author] had to face and go through. [She has] essentially written a book via journal entries that gives a message of hope. Congratulations on never giving up."

—Victor Cline, PhD, Emeritus Professor of Psychology, University of Utah.

"It is uncommon to be allowed inside another's heart. The depth of intimate feeling in the authentic voice of *My Darling From the Lions* may disturb you, inspire you, frighten you, or give you courage, but it will not leave you unchanged."

"Pornography and perversion are wicked weapons of mass destruction aimed at the assailable tendencies of youth by the master demon. For parents with addicted children there is reason take courage. For readers tainted by temptation or poisoned by pornography, it opens the raw wounds of emotional devastation you are causing in the lives of those who love you. For you deceived by the Father of Lies and ripped by the ragged thorns of homosexuality, there is hope. For any who have wondered why prophets urge the keeping of journals, now you know. For we who fear for our loved ones and struggle to defend ourselves against the onslaught of filth and perversions, *My Darling From the Lions* is a clarion call to greater vigilance and a swift retreat to the only true refuge and ultimate source of strength."

—Kieth Merrill, Academy Award winning filmmaker, writer and director of Legacy and The Testaments.

"This book offers an honest, hopeful, and poignant description of the pain families often experience when dealing with same-sex attraction. It gives a clear example that some young men do leave this challenge behind them. It also demonstrates how the love and support of others can be critical in this process. A book worth reading for anyone who seeks a more in-depth understanding of this difficult struggle."

—Jeffrey W. Robinson Ph.D.

"Words cannot convey my reaction to this truth-filled, powerful account, but I'll try. First, I was struck with the author's ability to be so honest with herself in her journal. I know that's the idea, but having that much self-knowledge and humility is not easy."

"I loved the book—the shorter beginning entries, the danger signs, the depth and passion with which the author shared the insights she gained. The progression from fear to faith, the constant but never tiresome expressions of gratitude, the ability to discuss sensitive topics, all were truly inspiring. The threads I especially enjoyed were Daniel's music, the quotes from scriptures and other sources, the golden cord of the husband Paul's supportive strength, the wonderful descriptions of family life, and the montage of Daniel's experience from childhood on."

"This book is for every parent. It raises the bar on active, loving, learning-by-doing parenting. These parents endured to see their son triumphant and Satan defeated. Thank you for this honest, timely sharing of your and—if the truth be told—so, so many families' story. I know this book can help all parents, not just those whose children have been grabbed by that ugly and evil facet of the internet."

—Fae Ellsworth, LMT, MFA, author, lecturer, teacher.

My Darling
from the Lions

My Darling
from the Lions

A boy falls to homosexuality.
A mother turns to God.
A family is changed forever.

Janice Barrett Graham

Edited by Camille G. Turpin

Contents

Editor's Note   *xi*

Author's Introduction   *xiii*

Part I   *5*

Part II   *37*

Part III   *55*

Part IV   *65*

Part V   *119*

Epilogue   *163*

Resources   *165*

Published by:
Tidal Wave Books
www.tidalwavebooks.com

Book design by Camille G. Turpin

Cover art by Andrew S. Graham

Copyright 2005 by Janice B. Graham
Printed in the United States of America

Library of Congress Cataloging-in-Publication Data available upon request

ISBN 0-9724770-3-9

Editor's Note

This book is made up of authentic journal entries written between the years 1994 and 2001 by an LDS woman living in Utah Valley. The entries were extracted from five different volumes containing roughly a thousand handwritten pages through which the story of a young man's struggle in overcoming homosexual thoughts and tendencies was intricately woven as told from his mother's perspective.

A great deal of repetition, common in spontaneous journal writing, has been edited out, hopefully without sacrificing an account of the gradual process of inner change in both Daniel and his mother. Graphics have been added to indicate passages of time spanning one month or longer. It is important to take note of the dates in order to realize the time involved in internalizing true principles and experiencing deep spiritual growth, all while dealing with the ups and downs of everyday family life.

Large amounts of material having to do with other aspects of the writer's life have also been left out, being irrelevant to the purposes of this book. We have included only those parts of the journals deemed important in establishing the setting, developing the characters, relating Daniel's experience particular to pornography and homosexuality, and conveying the spiritual growth experienced by both Daniel and his mother as a result.

Character names and some of the places mentioned in the journal entries have been changed both as a courtesy to the people involved, and also as an attempt to call attention away from specific individuals and on to universally applicable truths. Minor grammar, spelling, punctuation, and details were corrected, changed, or added for the purpose of clarity.

Author's Introduction

I have kept a journal for most of my life, never imagining for a moment that anything I was putting down would be publishable. All I knew was that my Heavenly Father saw fit to supply me with unlimited paper and ink as a merciful blessing to help me work through my questions, feelings, and experiences.

Amid a great deal of encouragement for this project, I was also told that sharing these particular journal writings may be too real and too raw, reopening unhealed wounds and causing pain for others. This is probably true. I imagine if each of us acknowledged and wrote down our honest feelings, our words would shock and dismay others and incriminate ourselves. But my belief is that we cannot make true and lasting progress unless we come out of the blindness of denial and face reality, however painful. In sharing this journal, my ultimate intention is not to cause discomfort, although that may occur, but to face truth, shed light on darkness, and open up the way to emotional health, knowledge and growth, peace, and joy.

Five years have passed since I went through what was up to that point the most traumatic trial of my life. Any well-meaning and conscientious mother whose child is wandering into what she considers to be dangerous paths will relate to the all-encompassing anxiety such a situation presents. In and around the many other areas of my life, I wrote in my journal some of what I felt and learned relating to the struggles of this child who for the purposes of this book I will call Daniel.

During the most intense period of Daniel's experience, I was surprised to find my own flaws and weaknesses as a human being and a mother becoming startlingly clear and meaningful for the first time in my life. Along with this inner illumination came a consciousness of the negative trends in the world increasing around me. I wished to share these stirring events but none of my efforts seemed to click and other book projects took precedence. All the while, developments were taking place in my community, church, and country that continued to confirm an urgent need to share my family's experiences.

One day as I was thinking about this difficult-to-tell story, my eyes rested on a box under my desk full of old journals I had dug up for another project. It occurred to me that there was a small chance I had already written this story down thoroughly enough to get its messages across. I ran this idea past Cami, my editor, who thought it might work. The very next day I began taking inventory, reading, cataloguing, making time lines and labels. I found that Daniel's story might indeed be woven like a single thread throughout five volumes. In that hope I started extracting, ending up with 300 pages. Cami helped me edit out half of those pages. This book is the result.

I am aware that the sociological issues this book addresses are intensely emotional, controversial, and political. My personal conviction is that homosexuality, whether in thought or deed, is spiritually and emotionally stagnating, and outside the laws of God, and therefore harmful to us as individuals or as a society. Like any attitude toward sexuality, I believe homosexual orientation is learned and may stem from a number of causes or combination of causes. Everyone who struggles with this issue is an individual who may have completely unique circumstances. But it is very important to note that in the last ten years, cases similar to Daniel's have greatly increased due to elements now prevalent in our society such as stereotypes promoted by the pervasive media, peer rejection and abuse, and internet pornography. The circumstances in Daniel's particular experience, if once rare or atypical, are rapidly becoming commonplace.

I am compelled to tell this story with three purposes in mind. The first is to provide hope and information for the growing number of individuals and families concerned with the issues of pornography addiction and homosexuality who wish to understand and root out such tendencies and ideologies from their personal lives and from society. Many people, for reasons of their own, do not face the fact that freedom from sexual obsessions and perversions is both a real and proximate possibility and a physically, emotionally, and spiritually preferable option. I know this idea may sound extremely harsh and cause pain to those who sincerely struggle with these issues, personally or in behalf of loved ones or friends, and my heart is drawn out in compassion. It is understandable that we experience feelings such as fear and anger when someone tells us that we have need to change something about ourselves for our own good especially when we think we have tried hard enough already. Whenever this happens we must seek the Spirit of Truth to discern whether there is any benefit to what we are hearing.

I am also aware that the story of Daniel's success in overcoming homosexual tendencies is only one story, but it is one undeniably true story. The degree of difficulty in reorienting sexual feelings depends on factors particular to each individual. The task may prove to be incredibly difficult for some and not so difficult for others. But the degree of the difficulty of a task has nothing to do with the rightness of striving toward it. It is up to each individual to decide if and when they wish to persevere in that effort.

The second even larger purpose in sharing this journal is to show the universality of exalting spiritual principles and the choice each of us have in applying them toward positive change.

The reason there is so much about Daniel's mother in this book, besides the fact that the nature of journal writing can be intensely personal and introspective, is to show that the same principles Daniel had to learn also applied to her. Each member of Daniel's immediate family was deeply affected by his dramatic fall and redemption. What we are privy to in this book is Daniel's mother's point of view. As she turns to God for solutions to her own problems, she becomes better able to be an effective instrument in helping her son.

Again, infinitely more important than the sociological issues this book addresses is the universal message of Christ's Atonement which can change our very natures no matter what our weaknesses or trials may be. I testify that we are all in need of a divine Savior. We will not grow into the kind of beings Heavenly Father would have us become unless we face this truth, painfully humbling though it may be. In this humbling process, we have the opportunity to learn exalting lessons in godly characteristics such as charity or pure, selfless love.

The last reason for this book concerns outward piousness vs. inward spirituality, and human relationships vs. our relationship to God. As I reviewed my old journals, I found that in between the lines was posed the intriguing question: Can we live our whole lives active in our church, whatever our religion, going obediently through the motions, and not have a deep, personal, guiding faith that will sustain us through any trouble? In the case of Mormons, or other Christians, can we live our lives participating in church culture, serving our fellow man, even ostensibly teaching and testifying of Jesus Christ, and yet remain oblivious to his true mission and the essential need for a personal relationship with him if we desire to dwell in the presence of God? The answer is yes. We can live in apparent obedience and gain no spiritual depth, if my own life proves a credible example.

Introduction

In this book I hope to illustrate the importance of examining our hearts to learn what truly moves and motivates us, and to show the benefits derived from efforts to purify those motivations as necessary. Here is a conversion story, not of new converts to religion but of life-long church-goers. Here is an honest, unaffected relating of the mountains and valleys every one of us must travel in order to understand our personal relationship with God apart from outward performances, the spiritual awareness of which makes all the difference between stagnating hypocrisy and the exciting inner progress God intends for us.

Some readers have expressed the wish that this book contained more of Daniel's thoughts and feelings during his experience—it is true that because this is his mother's journal we are given only second-hand glimpses of Daniel's personal journey. Being a journal keeper himself and a good writer, perhaps he will tell his story from his own point of view someday. But for now, *My Darling From the Lions* has his full support and approval.

Early in the development of this book, the real Daniel, almost 24, sat down one afternoon in my bedroom chair and read the manuscript straight through. When he was finished he had only one thing to say. "Mom, I had no idea at the time how deeply all of that affected you, how much pain it gave you and how much joy." Concerning this story, the thing that intrigued him was seeing it from his mother's perspective. The spiritual growth we experienced as individuals and as a family was nothing new to him—we discuss these miracles regularly. And the rest, the part about pornography and homosexuality, was ancient history. If you or someone you love struggles with these issues, it is our family's hope that it will soon be as ancient history in your life as well.

My Darling
from the Lions

Lord, how long wilt thou look on?
rescue my soul from their destructions,
my darling from the lions . . .
Yea, they opened their mouth wide . . .
Let them not say,
We have swallowed him up.

Psalms 35: 17, 21, and 25.

Part I

Lord, how long wilt thou look on?

September 6, 1994
Worried about Daniel (13). Is there no place for a good boy in this wicked world?

June 1, 1995
I just read about the three Nephites. I have worlds to learn about devotion to Christ.

For family home evening we decided to work on having charity—each of us has an assignment. Mine is to bear all things—and the funny thing is, I can't seem to bear even a feather of a frus tration. I am impatient and discouraged. I want everyone around me to be perfect—and they do just the opposite. Stuff, especially stuff out of place, drives me to distraction. The lawn mower sit- ting out in the rain, the waist-high heap of clippings from a week ago still sitting on the lawn, the bright orange extension cord mangling the front walkway, the brand new croquet set lit- tering the lawn, grandbaby furniture all over the living room, piano music all over the floor. I am a bundle of nerves and tears. One minute I resolve to cope, be nice, endure, bear it, and the next minute I am running off at the mouth with accusations and discouraging words. Back and forth, back and forth. I'm so ashamed of my weakness. The Lord gave us our weaknesses so they can become strengths. This is supposed to be my opportunity. But I can't find any strength anywhere. Just a sickness inside, flimsy and weak and limp. And it's raining again today.

Oh, how my pioneer ancestors would hate me.

June 9, 1995
I feel like my prayers were answered, or my hormones settled to a dull roar, or a little of both. I had the strong impression that I should ignore my children's bickering, the mess, etc., and refuse to contend with my children. I did this for two days. In that time I got a hold of myself and was able to think more clearly. I am reading Lynn Scoresby's *Bringing Up Moral Children*.

July 28, 1995
We couldn't learn much of anything if we didn't have each other. In *The 22 Laws of Wellness,* Greg Anderson says forgiveness applies to everything and to everyone, and all the time. This is what is meant by life being lived most abundantly as an adventure in forgiveness.

January 7, 1996
I am spending the day recovering from the flu. Everybody went to stake conference and sang in the family choir—I was sorry to miss. All five kids are spending the afternoon lounging, talking, laughing here in our room, clipping nails, reading, writing letters

to their missionary brother, while I sit here in bed sipping soda pop. Peace, relatively speaking. The kids are so bright, funny, full of intelligence and life and potential. Daniel (14) is on the window seat reading and highlighting a conference talk, preparing to give the family home evening lesson. I am chuckling because he has highlighted the entire page. Paul is beside me on the bed with his notebook computer studying his Book of Mormon lesson in preparation to teach the Gospel Doctrine class. Tonight we take Paige to the stake baptism preview. I think I'll feel well enough to go. Now Daniel is playing hymns on the piano in the living room. What have I done to deserve this? Thank you, Heavenly Father.

January 9, 1996
Lots of Young Women work today. Phone calls, meetings, Mutual, more phone calls. I am losing some girls—they just do not respond. My favorite scripture lately is 2 Corinthians 4:8–9. "We are troubled on every side, yet not distressed; we are perplexed, but not in despair; Persecuted, but not forsaken; cast down, but not destroyed." I want to memorize this, let it seep deep inside.

February 19, 1996
Hectic Monday as usual. Good home evening lesson—on self-control again. Wrote secret decoder letter to missionary Sam. We sang all verses of "Did You Think to Pray"—all four parts. Good kids, mostly happy, industrious, busy family involved in good things. Daniel (14) writing a story on the computer after having piano and trumpet lessons, Natalie (17) devouring a book

for a school assignment and making Young Women phone calls, Missy (11) writing in her journal, Shelly (11) reading aloud her last year's resolutions and discovering she had accomplished all but one, Paige (7) creating a treasure hunt for us. Is this heaven?

March 3, 1996
An awful Sunday—barely pulled off my responsibilities. A horrible self-loathing plagues me. A sensationless drift in the moonlit, body-temperature hot tub listening to Daniel and Paul play trumpet duets has calmed and revived me a little.

March 11, 1996
Worried about Daniel, how he seems determined to be a troublesome teen. I am determined to nip it in the bud! Paul is working hard at it, too. After an awful, willful evening Daniel finally softened—oh, he fights it so hard. It's like he has been taken over by an alien. Rude, thoughtless, disobedient. . . help! Now he and his dad are practicing trumpets.

March 14, 1996
Daniel has been more his old self. Seems like it's been an easier week. Natalie got accepted to BYU—we all went crazy with joy!

March 21, 1996
Daniel had a fun 15th birthday/swimming party. He seems to be suddenly growing up—caring about muscles and girls. Paul and I have talked a lot about him, about spending more time with him, lecturing less.

Ward temple night. It was so beautiful in the celestial room. I thought how amazing that this group of people are in this building promising these huge, deep, personal promises. What a refuge from the hard, unfeeling world. What a refined and gentle place. I want my home to be like this, too.

I woke up this morning sick and tired of negative thoughts, especially the kind that tear me, myself, down. I want to refuse to have them. I want a vacation from them. It's this always-wishing-to-do-better thing I have. Maybe I wish too hard to be perfect which isn't possible. I take too much time and energy beating myself up for every mistake, imperfection, flaw. Is there a corner of my brain I can store that wish in, work on it sub-consciously, while the rest of me is happy, positive, in control, and hopeful?

March 31, 1996
End of Sunday. End of March. What a month. I feel hashed. It was a monthful—mostly of church work. I want to get used to feeling the Spirit, so it's not so unusual and unsettling, so it's a happy thing. Saw President Hinckley at the Young Women conference.

April 22, 1996
Paul lost his job today. This was a shock but by the end of the day I was okay. It's not nearly so bad as last time. I am more humble this time. Maybe I have more faith. We've decided not to worry anyone about it.

April 23, 1996
Stake meeting. Hope I didn't sound negative. I am just tired. Talked to the bishop about Callie, a Laurel who is pregnant. He wants her out of Young Women, into Relief Society. I have to agree but my heart aches.

May 16, 1996
Does growing older mean coming to the truth about who you are? I used to think I could be anything—now I am beginning to accept me right where I am with no hope of changing. I'll never be the kind of person I want to be. I just don't have it in me, just can't do it. I'm starting to believe in my limitations. Too bad. Maybe I need to take a class, read a book. It's so hard to give up on oneself.

September 1, 1996
It's Labor Day but Paul is working to load a new computer program at his new office. Made bread and cinnamon rolls. Last night in the tent on the lawn we started reading a new book aloud, *The Light in the Forest.* Daniel is 15, just like True Son in the book. President Hinckley says four simple things to do for family are teach goodness, work together, read good books together, and pray together. Most recently, *The Yearling* had a profound effect on us, though it took six months to read it aloud.

September 5, 1996
Natalie's troubles at college (scheduling classes, choosing her major) have really affected me. Troubles at church, too. I'm feeling paranoid, insecure, and worried about my children, my job as their mother, my church job, my faults and offenses, my weaknesses.

I want to elevate myself, my thinking, my outlook, my opinions of others, my service to others, my contribution, the quality of my surroundings, however simple. How can I do this—for real? How can I rise above everything petty and untidy and impure? How can I like myself even though I am getting older and not making the progress I hoped for in my character and qualities? Maybe it doesn't matter what we do as long as we keep busy in anything positive. Maybe I expect too much.

September 9, 1996
Had a long discussion with Daniel over a small mistake. I over-reacted as usual. But we had a great talk in the end and lots of love. Daniel needs tons of approval and more space.

October 6, 1996
So discouraged about the girls in Young Women. Another girl is pregnant and her mother is celebrating, as far as I can tell. After going to her baby shower (fancy house, fancy gifts and photos) I fell apart. No one seemed to be crying for her—for the loss, for the missed youth, for purity, for the temple—that I guess I thought I had to. I wept for two days. Everything seemed so futile and hopeless. I think my heart was breaking for this girl. We had to go rehearse at the temple for the dedication choir and I was so discouraged I could hardly go in. At the last minute I realized a simple truth. I am not allowed to be discouraged. So I went in. "And hearts are brave again and arms are strong. Alleluia!"

October 9, 1996
Parent-teacher conference for Daniel was full of glowing reports.

October 20, 1996
Paul put on old family videos of four years ago when all our children were still home. They have all grown so fast lately. Daniel grew four inches this last year! I'm missing my young family. And missing my big kids who are gone gone gone. I have to adjust.

November 1, 1996
It seems the last few weeks have been extra-full of laughter and love. I am ultra-sensitive and greedy for happy moments.

On Wednesday we heard Sam was being transferred to the mission home, called to be a proselyting assistant to the president. I never dreamed! He has worked really hard—and then he has always had that people personality. There is no stopping him when he is committed! What a lot he has learned on his mission! He loves to be at the very heart of things, a born leader. Five more months.

Daniel is such a good boy but lately a girl who is a senior is interesting to him and we've had phone problems. Finally, after he talked until midnight one night (even after he made a deal to keep conversations to a half hour on school nights) we took the phone away. It worked. He's been really excited about the French horn. Practicing nonstop! Band concert Wednesday night.

November 4, 1996
I was useless this past weekend with Paul gone. It had been so long since we have been apart—I'm spoiled. Finally, he's home. We went out for a fancy dinner to celebrate Sam's success and

went to see a movie, *Phenomenon,* which we loved and decided held the key to the universe and the purpose of life and eternity: Heavenly Father, who knows everything, has all knowledge and desires to share it, but we have to learn, line upon line.

November 10, 1996
Sunday. Seven meetings today. Tired out. I bet pioneer great-great-grandpa Ellsworth never got tired out. Have to build stamina.

December 3, 1996
I arranged a big holiday party and then stressed out about it. Paul took over and it was a warm, happy time. Got a few decorations up—evergreen garlands and candles. There were all kinds of musical numbers from serious to silly. Mom and Dad, a missionary companion of Sam's who just got home, all the kids, and some of Natalie's college friends came. Singing, viola, banjo, guitar, and piano, even karaoke! Grandson Logan was the hit of the party singing Primary songs—and not even two years old yet! It was a wild and crazy night. Daniel was showing off terribly—at 15 he is as cute as ever, getting handsome and what a ham. He and his favorite cousin Chase surprised us with a piano and vocal duet, "Yesterday." Natalie sang "Memories," Jason sang "If," Lindsay sang "Mary Let Me Hold Her Baby," and Paul was a perfect host. The twins did their funny "Jingle Bells" piano duet. When can we do this again?

December 19, 1996
So busy. The whiteboard is filled with daily activities so we can keep them straight—two and three things every night. We're almost done. The month of December is filled with deadlines. Mostly I've been doing Young Women stuff. We did fruit baskets

again this year and it took me many trips to deliver the stragglers during the week. Then we had our Santa's workshop we've been planning all year. The two girls who said they'd do the toys for their Laurel project didn't do anything. So I was sewing beanbags and buying paint. The Mutual kids sanded, painted, turned, stuffed, and sewed after watching a touching video of Romanian orphans, neglected and toyless. Afterwards, the bishop called me in his office and released me. I was caught a little off guard and wept. How can you turn off all the energy, love, worry, and thought so suddenly? All the girls passed before my eyes. And then the thoughts of, Did I do my best? Was it enough? Could I have done more? It's been a long, full three years.

January 15, 1997
A happy taco supper. So nice to be more organized. After dinner Daniel read aloud to us from *The Prince and the Pauper*. He has been doing the reading lately—we like how he does it—a great reader. I did my run in the snow today. Hard going. Feet slid with every step.

January 16, 1997
Tended Logan today. Baked bread, cleaned out the pantry and some kitchen cupboards. Natalie called and chatted my ear off which I loved. Talked to my first counselor Joanne and was sorry to hear that another of the Laurels is having to get married. That makes eight girls in a three-year period who chose to ignore everything they've been taught. It is discouraging and tragic. It also makes me more determined than ever to teach my children—and keep teaching.

January 27, 1997
For family night we had "Daniel night." We watched his fantastic

band video and then Paul took him practice driving at the church parking lot. Yesterday was not so good—a conflict with Daniel over phone use. Too many hours spent! He seemed sad. But brightened up today. A good boy.

February 4, 1997
O.J. Simpson was found guilty in the civil trial. At last a measure of justice is served. This world has such devious ways of twisting the truth, calling good evil, and evil good.

February 10, 1997
Daniel didn't get to check out anything at the library because he didn't come when it was time to go. Typical 15. Never thought Daniel would be like this. We are always waiting for him.

February 15, 1997
Daniel came home from a seven-stake dance, and said, "I'm starting to get too cool . . ." He has such a mop of great hair which he doesn't want me to cut too short, and nice dark eyebrows. He's been a good son lately.

February 16, 1997
No school tomorrow so we finished reading *The Prince and the Pauper* which we all loved. Daniel and I stayed up late talking and laughing. Then we video taped Paul snoring! Ha-ha.

Daniel is being difficult a lot of the time, talking on the phone for hours on end, being mean to the girls, sneering and growling, stomping and yelling. The teens have hit him full force. And I had hoped it would never happen.

February 19, 1997

Trouble with Daniel. He didn't come home after school, then finally showed up an hour and a half late. Then he didn't call for a ride after the basketball game either and showed up a few hours later. We told him all he has to do is call and let us know his plans. He doesn't seem willing to do this. Teenagers think they have no connections, like they fell from the sky, landed here, and are just owed everything they need and want. Daniel is basically a good boy with strong basic values. But he is a selfish teenager, thoughtless of others. What to do? I want to give him more space but he takes miles when I do this. And he storms like a child when things don't go his way—like when he's on the computer and one of us has to use it. Even if his dad has to do actual work, Daniel won't get off. It's crazy. And he won't talk to us. He just clams up. That's the most frustrating part.

February 23, 1997

Went to a wonderful fireside with the whole family about the importance of happy families. Filled with the Spirit. A Church video and four great talks. Paul and I can improve greatly in our patience and attention toward the kids. They need to get along better. Daniel is the worst problem right now. He stayed in my room for an hour complaining and arguing about calling a girl after 10:30 (I said no). He stays up late every night and has been sleeping through our family morning devotional and being tardy for school. He is obsessed with this senior girl who seems to have lots of problems. I need to help him get more involved in other things. French horn lessons? Clogging?

March 4, 1997

Parent-teacher conference at the high school. Daniel is a good boy—not perfect but a good kid. High grades.

Part I

March 13, 1997

Signed Daniel up for summer music workshop at BYU.
Expensive but worth it. Natalie so enjoyed it the years she went.

March 15, 1997

Shopping for Daniel's 16th birthday. File cabinet, piano music,
CDs, and clothes.

March 16, 1997

Sunday. Daniel had a nice birthday. Everybody came over—so
noisy. We sang every birthday song we know and got louder and
louder. Daniel is really growing up. I think he will get taller still.
Highlight of the day was Daniel's excellent talk in Church on
service. He's so excited to get his driver's license.

March 26, 1997

Here we are in Washington State to pick up Sam after two whole
years. We visited the mission home. Daniel was Mr. Personality
and totally won Sister Ethington's heart. She kept saying things
like, "He's not like other teenagers! Daniel, you must be an
artist—you notice all my pictures. Nobody does that! I want my
grandsons to be just like you. You need to come on your mission here!"

March 28, 1997

Mostly in the car today. Seeing some sights. Lots of time to
read, doze, visit. Sam is a little quiet and serious. Daniel is loud,
silly, and obnoxious but we are putting up with him the best we
can. He provides occasional comic relief.

April 6, 1997

Busy with General Conference. So fun to have all my children in one place. Families are, or can be so volatile. Sometimes I feel the bonds and values that hold us together are so fragile. A family is only as strong as the commitment of its members. I am feeling the impact of my kids growing up. It is hard to swallow.

April 12, 1997
At Wal-Mart I picked out polo shirts for the family photo. What a problem to get all eleven together! In between everyone's various activities we met for ten minutes at the elementary school where they were doing a photo fundraiser. It was really pretty ridiculous all the things happening on this one night. Dates, Scout meetings, parties, wedding receptions. At 5 P.M. Daniel was ordained a priest by his brother Sam here at the house.

April 17, 1997
Played tennis with kids. Daniel wouldn't come.

April 18, 1997
More trouble with Daniel. He is acting so spoiled and childish.

April 20, 1997
For some reason I was nervous and uneasy all day. I'm disappointed in myself and everyone else. Life isn't going my way. I am struggling to turn my attitude around from dissatisfied to grateful—quit thinking I'm a failure because my kids aren't doing exactly what I wish. I am stuck in my own muddy, sticky expectations of how life ought to be. I'm stuck but I'm lost, too, wandering in my troubled thoughts, looking for a comforting place to rest. I need to rely on Paul. I need to cast my burdens on the Lord. I need to repent and clean up my act—purify my heart, love and serve, quit being selfish and small, count my blessings, which are myriad.

April 22, 1997

It seems every day we have a problem with Daniel. But he took a walk last night and then slipped his dad and me notes under our bedroom door. They were so good and sweet and comforting I taped them to my mirror. This gives me hope.

I feel like some terrible, awful things are happening to our family, like it's falling apart, like all the past was for nothing—all the happy times, the struggles, the home evenings, the singing together, all the piano lessons, all the vacations, all the good, stable, strong, secure feelings are fading away as if it all never happened. I'm faced with a new sort of family with all kinds of problems and tension and complications. Everyone is so complex now, going in their own directions rather than in the directions I planned, taught, hoped for. Those simple days when we were all together, unified, only wanting to be with each other, happiest all together, are gone. It's just too awful. I'm losing the thing I've most worked at and cared about my whole life. My career, as I've known it, is disintegrating. Oh, I miss it. I'm going to have to work harder at letting go.

They are not mine anymore. I'll think of them as different people. I'm not in charge anymore. They're on their own. I'm so scared I can't look. I feel myself closing off. It's the only way to survive it; it hurts so much.

It's weird. I feel like in the past few months I've gone from the top of the world to the depths of despair. Everything seemed to be going so great—our kids doing so well—now I'm buried in worries and disappointments and crises. All in the walls of my own home. It all has to do with Daniel.

April 27, 1997

Things are better. Daniel, for one, has been good and calm ever since he wrote those letters to his dad and me. We have been able to give him some privileges, he's been busy with the marching band and planning scout leadership camp. He's filling out job applications.

May 1, 1997

Daniel made drum major! Just like his big brother.

May 9, 1997

These days, I mostly worry about my kids' emotional safety and whether they're learning responsibility, and if they'll crash driving on the freeway. I worry who they'll marry and if it'll work and what they'll do to make a living. I worry what kind of people they will turn out to be and if I've done my job. In other words, I've learned that I no longer have control over these grown-up ones and all I can do now is pray.

What a blessing that my kids seem to have a measure of common sense, testimonies of the gospel, desires to do right and improve themselves, interest in many things, and a loyalty to family. It is a humbling, sobering thing to consider the job I've done so far as a parent.

May 15, 1997

On our date at the movies we got a call on the cellular. Daniel wrecked the van into a tree on his way down the canyon from playing trumpet for a Scout thing. He had a bloody nose and was crying, very upset. It turned out that the steering may have been the problem, plus Daniel being in too much of a hurry to get home. I said over and over that I didn't think Daniel was ready to drive in the canyon, especially at night, but he argued and begged and complained until we gave in. I even said, "I'm afraid—I don't want you to go." When we offered to drive him, he scoffed. He even had a ride with a leader and refused it. He said he just wanted to show us he could do it. Sam said it was a miracle the van didn't flip, after looking at the scene. From now on I'm going to be firm in things that I feel strongly about. It's so hard though, when Daniel freaks out about what he calls his "horrible life in which he is not allowed to do anything."

June 8, 1997
Daniel went to Petersons' and got his hair buzzed. I think he looks pretty tough. He is a cute boy. He sold 27 pizzas over the phone for the band fundraiser.

June 16, 1997
Had a big blow-up with Daniel who said he was going to play practice but instead went to a girlfriend's.

July 12, 1997
We all went to Lagoon for Paul's big company party. It turned out to be the nicest time ever there—cool weather, everyone in good spirits, riding all the rides, enjoying each other. We had a great day and laughed and sang the entire way home.

July 13, 1997
Sunday. Had watermelon on the deck. Paige had us play silly games. We started reading aloud *David Copperfield*—kids falling asleep. Put girls to bed and then sat around with Daniel, Natalie, and Sam who was restringing Natalie's guitar. Nice.

July 15, 1997

Daniel did a stupid thing. We let him take the van to Mutual and afterwards he took it to see friends and got home late. He knows the rules but the present temptations completely take over. No driving once again. This kid may never drive.

July 20, 1997

Sunday. We went to a fireside for everyone participating in the Church's Sesquicentennial spectacular. Elder Holland spoke at the Richards Building. This is a big deal we are in, the biggest production the Church has ever done in terms of the number of people involved. It's thrilling to sing in the 1,700-person choir. I'm really happy that all seven of my children are experiencing this.

July 24, 1997

Pioneer Day—Sesquicentennial! I got up early with the pioneer spirit in my heart and made cowboy cake for our annual cousins tennis/breakfast party at the park. Got everybody up except Daniel and had fun on the courts. Then we all took naps and got ready and went to the stadium with a little picnic. What a huge crowd. Sixty thousand, all sold out. Everyone said it was indeed spectacular. Fireworks, dancing water fountains, dancers, music, singing, covered wagons and horses, pioneers. The best part was the 3,600 missionaries who marched in at the end, eight abreast, filling the whole perimeter of the BYU football field. They were so excited and the crowd went wild. I hope the kids remember it forever.

August 4, 1997

The big excitement today was Daniel getting a job at a silkscreening T-shirt place. It has been a problem all summer trying to find him a job. Toward evening Paige was crying. It turned out she was afraid to be left home alone with Daniel because he is so mean to her. So a family discussion ensued. Daniel was belligerent and defensive but in the end he admitted there was room for improvement.

August 23, 1997
Last night Paul and I went to Daniel's high school band party to chaperone—a six-hour marathon party at the rec center. They roller-skated, and played hockey and basketball nonstop. It was fun to see Daniel in action. He has enough personality for the entire group.

August 24, 1997
Sunday. In sacrament meeting Daniel sang with a group of ten friends a gorgeous arrangement of "Come Thou Fount of Every Blessing" that they had practiced really hard. Daniel sang away at the high tenor part without looking down at the music— just smiling confidently out toward the congregation. Many people wept.

In the evening we went to the high school marching band concert in the park as always. Daniel had a solo in one number and also played in a trio.

So blessed and proud and comforted tonight by my good boy.

August 25, 1997
First day of school for Daniel—11th grade!

August 26, 1997
Went to high school Back-to-School night where the band played. We fixed Daniel's schedule, trading around seminary so he could be in AP Spanish. I have great hopes for Daniel's high school career—lots of high grades, scholarship opportunities, leadership experiences, and plenty of social fun. He is loving being in the clogging dance group.

August 31, 1997
As we were having family home evening, Sam and Rachel came over to show off THE RING! It's official! Another temple wedding. Everyone is pleased and happy. It looks like a good match.

September 14, 1997
Homecoming date for Daniel—we waited up for him until 2 A.M. and then talked with him until 3 about our midnight curfew. Exhausted and worried.

September 24, 1997
Daniel's parent-teacher conference was mostly good but one thing was upsetting. He got caught faking his book report. I can't believe he could do that. I was so embarrassed. Besides that, I had been trying to get him to read *The Last of the Mohicans* for weeks. Anyway, Paul and I tried to approach Daniel in a nonhysterical manner.

September 25, 1997
I told Daniel he couldn't go to a clogging class because he needed to read his book (which he talked to the teacher about and apologized, etc.). He said he promised to finish it when he got home. But when he got home he had to do other homework. Hmmm.

September 26, 1997
Paul and I were going to go on our date tonight but decided we better stay home and "babysit" 16-year-old Daniel who wanted to go to a football game but couldn't because we said he had to finish his infernal BOOK. We ordered take-out and watched videos. Daniel finished his book and we discussed it. Phew.

October 4, 1997
Daniel polished up his "conscience-imposed" book report. (His teacher said he didn't have to redo it but he did anyway.) I have to remind him every day about English homework. I got him a copy of *Moby Dick* that he has to read next.

October 6, 1997
I read an article in *Reader's Digest* about guilt. I agree that I need to rid myself of "ghosts"—old, inconsequential little mistakes that give me shivers regularly—but I think some kinds of guilt regarding really important things are signals that we don't have our priorities straight. I will continue to use that kind to do better.

Paul and I rode the bus with the band kids to Daniel's band competition in Payson. I worried about the three girls fending for themselves for the evening, but they are old enough now. It was fun to see the band in action and get to know people. Daniel was the noisiest boy on the bus. We told him to keep it down numerous times. But on the way home as we approached the school he kept yelling, "Second speed bump, everyone!" We didn't know what he meant by this huge announcement until the bus went over the school parking lot's second speed bump and Daniel proceeded to lead the entire bus in the most rousing rendition of a school song I ever heard!

October 7, 1997

My family is changing again. It is such an endless task to keep up with growing children, to keep relationships alive and happy and healthy. That is a daily task. I'm tired. So many relationships. So complex. So demanding. So worth it.

October 9, 1997

Last night I had one of my dark times. Everything looked so hopeless. I felt trapped and totally ineffectual to change my situation. It was mostly the condition of the house that was discouraging me. It is in need of attention. I complained and despaired. Paul listened and attempted to console. He is so patient.

Today I did better. The kids are out of school for UEA break. They worked hard on the house. Daniel said he likes *Moby Dick* and can't put it down—at least compared to *Last of the Mohicans.* Ha-ha.

October 14, 1997

Daniel handed me $170 this morning. He is paying for his own tux for choir. Good thing he has a job. It won't hurt him.

October 17, 1997

Tonight Daniel and I watched a video of *The Crucible,* which he just read for school. Horrible, ignorant, prideful, self-righteous, small-minded people. I can't believe how they thought back then. So glad Paul will be home tomorrow, my rudder and sail, my balance. Daniel comforted me, talking and listening tonight. He is really growing up lately.

October 21, 1997

Daniel helped me move furniture today. He was so cute about it.

Part I

October 31, 1997

A wedding is a big thing. My emotions are ricocheting all over the place. It's also been a busy time of year with three birthdays and Halloween. Plus Daniel had band and choir concerts. He was handsome in his tux, but he still has the little boy face that stole my heart sixteen years ago.

December 2, 1997

My children are all so good and sweet. What more could I want?

December 8, 1997

It was the big choir concert at the high school tonight, plus the cloggers. Daniel was cute and clogged up a storm.

December 10, 1997

We were upset with Daniel because his grades are not as good as usual. So we had a talk—he cried his heart out—and reached the conclusion that he has never really had to work for A's and finally with these honors classes, he has to study. So we are having study time every night now.

December 30, 1997

The last holiday weeks were so busy I never wrote. It was awful. I lost all balance and equilibrium trying to be all things to all people. I thought service was supposed to make you happy and fulfilled. Instead, I've felt overextended and buried in neverending work. I guess the things I was spending time on were not important—which were candy-making, card making and sending, gift buying, holiday decorating, sewing, and wrapping.

The best things, the good things about this Christmas were the concerts, the ancestral family Christmas story I dug up that everyone loved, the extended family parties on both sides, and the opportunity to be of a little genuine service to a family that had to move the day before Christmas Eve. We helped clean their house and drove them to a relative's house in Sandy where they will spend Christmas. It didn't seem like a sacrifice at all. It just needed to be done. I was grateful to get a little relief from all the meaningless stuff. This year the kids have been so demanding and inflexible, resisting any slight change in tradition.

For Christmas I made a little booklet called "Who are my Ancestors?" which I had been wanting to do all year. Daniel did the illustrations and I typed up some interesting short stories to introduce our pioneer ancestors to this rising generation. The whole family helped with the printing, sorting, and binding and we gave them to all the cousins at the family party.

January 5, 1998
We laughed a lot tonight and read *David Copperfield* curled up in front of the cozy fire sipping hot chocolate. We are at the part where David made it to Aunt Betsy's and we met Mr. Dick.

Our New Year's Day holiday was a little hectic but we celebrated to everyone's satisfaction. I liked our traditional ice-skating outing best.

January 28, 1998
The big buzz is the mess in the White House. I don't even like to write about it, except to say it's all embarrassing and disgusting.

Part I

And yes, I think we should be able to choose leaders who are exemplary and virtuous.*

February 2, 1998
Everyone got up for devotional. I read Moroni 7:42–48 and we discussed how charity is more than giving time, money, things, or even kindness. It's a change of heart, a softening and purifying, an open, generous love for everyone, a radiating of good feelings to all, the pure love of Christ. We decided that the first kind of charity, the outward actions, is easy. The second kind is very difficult. Cease to be critical, cease to compete and compare. Be patient, give the benefit of the doubt, appreciate people for their efforts, be humble. I'm going to have to get this before I can teach my lesson next Sunday!

I was feeling discouraged yesterday as I sat in Relief Society (for the first time in years because of callings in Young Women and nursery). I found myself thinking everyone was missing the most important points. But then I realized it was ME who was missing the most important point of all. I am not smarter than anyone else. I was being proud and critical! How depressing.

February 4, 1998
Spent all afternoon and evening decorating and setting up for the high school band banquet. Everything went fine. It's going to be a challenge to be the band parent association presidents next year. I hope we make a difference. It will be a big year for Daniel being the drum major.

---

*President Clinton and Monica Lewinsky.

February 8, 1998

A big day—my first lesson in Relief Society, everyone over for lasagna dinner (left over from band banquet), and New Beginnings where the twins played "Families Can Be Together Forever" on their flutes. Oh, and choir practice after church. As we were eating cookies after choir practice, I thanked a sister for participating in my lesson and she proceeded to politely inform me that she had researched a piece of information I had given and found it to be untrue. I was stunned. I apologized and thanked her again. Later, Paul said she was wrong but didn't want to argue with her. And Daniel, who had been standing there, too, said he thought she was extremely rude. But I was left feeling the sharp criticism. It felt as if I had blundered through the whole thing. Paul talked me through it. We had a long discussion about perfectionism, humility, and forgiveness. In the end, I had to put it all out of my mind, having "punished" myself quite enough.

February 9, 1998

I worked all day at avoiding thoughts of my lessons and did pretty well.

February 10, 1998

My fear and self-condemnation is wearing off. I need to stand firm. Be a good friend to myself.

February 26, 1998

Daniel got his patriarchal blessing. I think Daniel is a very good boy. What struck me most about his blessing was that it mentioned his faith several times, that his faith would get him through many challenges. I was warmed by Daniel's goodness.

March 2, 1998

I am still feeling strange. It's so tempting to give in to these little feelings of fear and doubt and weakness. It's confusing because lately I've been trying so hard to be charitable in my thoughts and doing a lot of service for others. I'm afraid of making mistakes and forgetting things (like I forgot my mother-in-law's birthday yesterday). I can't forgive myself. I'm tormented by all my failures. I haven't felt bad like this in a long time. It helps to think about others and do ordinary things.

March 5, 1998

Paul brought me a dozen multicolored roses. Am I blessed or what? I am feeling better today, trying to channel my thoughts. I am doing good things, maybe not as good as others, not as showy, not as far-reaching, but I'm doing good. I have a family who needs my love and support and encouragement, a house that needs running, plans and chores that need doing. Lindsay needs me to tend Logan and Lacy so she can finish college. I have to do my running to keep sane. I have to be cheerful and pleasant for my husband. I have to keep my kids healthy and fulfill all their needs. And we're doing a lot of work on the house. It's a lot.

March 8, 1998

I gave my second Relief Society lesson today—on the Atonement, which was so difficult. The sisters are just a blur. I feel kind of detached. I only had twenty minutes and could not cover even half of the material. I don't think I'm doing this calling right. I want so much to rid myself of all ego and let the Spirit teach me what points to bring out and how to portray the message. The whole Atonement is difficult to grasp completely, maybe impossible. I don't have a clue what the sisters are really thinking.

Their comments help a little and are generally excellent and insightful. Maybe I should just use the time up with their comments. I'll try that. Just guide a big discussion next time.

March 10, 1998
I got really fed up with Daniel and his obsession with the computer today. I really lost it. I think he got the message. I'm just through with his rudeness and disobedience. He ignores everything for hours when he gets on there and loses track of time, disregarding any rules or compromises. So it's over. It's been the cause of so much frustration. Our biggest problem lately.

March 11, 1998
Paul and I took Daniel to Natalie's Women's Chorus concert at BYU and out to eat. The concert was awesome and Daniel is back. When we disentangle him from the computer he miraculously returns to us in all his delightful personality.

March 16, 1998
Daniel's 17th birthday. I got my run in early and took off to the grocery store and mall. Picked out some nice clothes for Daniel, which he desperately needs. He wears his clothes to shreds. Had a nice birthday dinner—everybody came.

March 23, 1998
Somehow we got the entire family together for our annual family photo again at the elementary school. It was a madhouse with bribes of pizza and banana splits afterwards. An outright miracle to have everybody together, all in happy moods. Had a nice, long, fun visit. Good sports all around.

March 30, 1998
For family night we helped Daniel with his art portfolio and had ice cream. He has a wonderful talent. All those years of practicing have paid off. He can really draw! Confidence and experience have made him bold.

April 1, 1998
Our family photo turned out fine. Is this a happy time? I better savor it.

Part II

rescue my soul from their destructions

April 20, 1998

Something awful has happened. It's bad. How dumb can parents be? Last night we found out that Daniel has been lying and sneaking to look at trashy pictures on the internet. Evidently he has been doing this off and on for at least a year. My heart aches to put it in writing. Thoughts include guilt and disgust that Paul and I would allow access (easy access I learned) to that horrid, low, cheap material in our very home—which I've spent my life trying to fill with refinement and beauty—and incredulity that we didn't know Daniel was doing it. I am in shock. I don't even know if he has told us the worst of it. I can't trust my darling boy. His innocence is ruined, spoiled. It's a disaster.

I guess I could sob all day but instead I've got to concentrate on how to overcome this ugly problem. First, face it. Don't rationalize that it's not as bad as all that. It's probably worse than I imagine. Second, get rid of the internet. Third, get Daniel to go to the bishop. This is embarrassing and humiliating for us all but it's the only way Daniel can start repenting. Fourth, renew efforts to teach correct principles with regular family home evenings and father's interviews, etc. Fifth, renew efforts to be diligent, devoted parents. Make children the most important thing—don't get distracted. PAY ATTENTION.

I just talked to Paul on the phone at the office. He's going to try to spend more time with Daniel and focus on him. Maybe do some good things—camping, skiing, whatever. Something exciting. Spend a lot of time together. Get close. Get to know each other better.

I'm worried sick at what lies ahead. Is it going to be a nightmare? Worse than my wildest fears? I think yes. I hate this world we live in.

April 21, 1998
I just ripped out two pages of this journal because I wrote about Daniel's problem and I don't want it for posterity.

I suddenly woke up this morning at 4 A.M. and spoke the word "nightmare." And then I knew it wasn't one. It was real life. I couldn't sleep so I went in the living room wrapped in a blanket and wept and prayed. I got some ideas about what I can do. I feel a deep heartsickness. I am shattered. We talked and cried a lot yesterday and I read Daniel's detailed everyday journals and found the problem to be worse than imagined. I don't know if Daniel can change. Paul says he can. I'm so afraid.

I am ridding my home of every evil influence. After reading Daniel's meticulously kept journals I see that I was blind and desensitized to what my kids (especially my young, artistic, absorbent, sensitive, harrassed-all-his-life son) were being exposed to. Daniel is prone to be obsessive, and got obsessed with the wrong things. We will have to get help. Bit by bit, step by step. It was so gradual. He got in deeper and deeper. I wasn't paying attention. I failed to protect my son. This is disastrous and may have eternal consequences for us all. The devil, indeed, leads us carefully down to hell.

This is a hard time. I'm getting rid of the TV, videos, everything. I'm moving Daniel upstairs to the old nursery that we've been using as an office so he can be closer to us. From now on this is a G-rated house. We'll spend more time with each other, talking, teaching, learning, helping, working, caring. Paul is supportive of these ideas. I am shocked that there is so much to change. We do watch too much stuff that is not so good. Paul and I are sickened by our complacence. We've grown lazy with our children. Is all lost? How ruined are they? Paul says it's not too late but I am sick at heart. A wake-up call, to put it mildly. I have committed crimes against my innocent children by allowing bad influences in my home. I can't believe it.

April 24, 1998
We finally got in touch with the bishop. He was concerned, supportive, and encouraging. In the last few days I have cried a lot, despaired and imagined the worst for Daniel's future. But Paul and the bishop say all can be worked through and made right. It is not too late for my sweet, good boy.

We've worked hard all week. Daniel has hated the changes we've made. One night he sobbed and moaned in his room. But I think he's getting used to the way things are going to have to be. I've tried to break it to him bit by bit. So far we've gotten rid of all the videos except family and church. Even the harmless ones are a waste of time, taking time away from important things. We've got him moved into the room across from us so we can keep a close eye on him. Today I'd better censor his journals. He can't bear to throw them away so we agreed to tear out the pages with bad stuff. I guess I have to do it*. I've been putting it off. It's so hurtful to my heart and spirit. And, oh, my poor son. I can't believe he has seen and thought and written these things. My whole understanding has opened up. Oh why couldn't I see and be warned before this happened? Why do we believe we are safe? I guess no one is safe. We have to be diligent in avoiding even the appearance of evil, even a hint of it.

Paul was reading the other night, got up and threw his book in the trash. This is our new attitude. Next, we'll get rid of a few books and some records and CDs. Even if it's not bad, it's too much—obsessive, distracting, numbing.

We think Daniel needs some professional help concerning his obsessive behaviors. The bishop says that any obsessiveness is indeed a problem and we should do something about it. The point is, you have to know your children, what kind of personalities they have, how much and what kinds of attention they need and activities they can benefit from, what they are thinking, what stage they are going through, how things they see and hear are affecting them. You can only do this if you take the time to really focus on your child, discuss, listen, think, ponder. Put your heart into it. Don't get distracted. It's too dangerous a world.

Things are changing around here. I pray for guidance and understanding and balance. I am humiliated, humbled to the dust. I think my lack of attention and thought to my children has been the worst sin of my life. I feel like a criminal. I am motivated,

*In the end Daniel censored his own journals, crossing out offensive material.

determined to clean out my mind and my home of every bad or useless thing.

I have so much to do. But it is all cast aside. Nothing matters but the physical and spiritual needs of my family. Physical, because it's always necessary, and spiritual, because it is called to my attention.

April 26, 1998
This is sad: It wasn't until I had nowhere to go and no one to turn to that I turned to the bishop, a thing I have never done in my whole life. It seemed too simple, I didn't think he'd be able to help. But he did. He opened the understanding of my heart and taught me. He did have solutions.

These are some of the things the bishop taught or reminded me of:

☐ When thoughts get all confused and conflicting, go back to basic truths. These are: Heavenly Father lives, Jesus lives, and They love me.

☐ The deepest answers to our problems are not in books of popular psychology but in the doctrines of Jesus Christ. Quick fixes are shallow and world-based. Examining our spirits is the most direct and effective solution. True doctrine will change behavior faster and better than any amount of talking can. (Both mine and Daniel's behavior.)

☐ Children are ours eternally, but are even more our Heavenly Father's and He loves them.

☐ Life isn't going to go along exactly as planned even if we're keeping the commandments. Bad things will happen—that's the nature of this life. It's how we react, it's what we learn, it's what we become that's important.

☐ Don't give up. Children need to see parents enduring, coping, crying some, loving.

☐ The Atonement is not just for those repenting of sins. It's for anyone who suffers the effects of sin and sorrow, for understanding, strength, inspiration, forgiveness . . .

☐ Teach children to recognize the promptings of the Holy Ghost. They have their agency—we can't force them to be good, we can't be there with them always or read their minds. So our only hope is to teach them to listen and discern. If they haven't learned this or have forgotten what it feels like, they need to repent and start over. (Paul and I are doing this ourselves.)

☐ Concentrate on the child, not the wrongdoing. (This is why I had the meltdown. I totally stressed out about the evil thing and forgot the goodness and potential of my child.)

☐ We are all thrown together, in families, in wards, in neighborhoods, all flawed and human, impossibly imperfect. So all we can do is try our best to help, serve, get along, and forgive each other.

May 3, 1998

It's so symbolic that at this point in our lives we are making improvements on our worn-out house. We've been slowly painting walls, doors, and ceilings since January. Things are in a state of organized disorganization—getting worse before it gets better, which is the same state our spirits are in. The condition of the house adds stress but on the other hand is a sort of reprieve from the worry and intensity of our long, heart-felt discussions. To paint a wall or clean out a closet is a welcome respite.

It's so strange, or maybe good, that in the last week we've had in-depth discussions or epiphanies with each individual child about their own particular concerns. Paige had to learn consequences for not being on time, Shelly was caught up in expensive clothes and envying friends and being tempted to see inappropriate movies to be popular. Missy was upset by people expecting her to be perfect. And our discussions with Daniel continue, always taking a new direction, taking in new aspects of repentance, good vs. evil, changing our hearts, and figuring out what we need to be thinking about.

I ask myself over and over, where have I been? Wrapped up in my own projects, in wanting things for my house, in too much entertainment, in my own problems and needs and wants. I've just been going through the motions. I'm actually grateful all this has happened. My focus is changed. I feel sad for my past wrongs and laziness and inattention. But I am so glad to be humbled down and renewed. When I'm not sorrowing for my faltering I am light and happy inside to be headed in the right and better and more refined direction.

It's almost as if I have been waiting for a test, for a trial, for something to shake me into action.

June 2, 1998
I haven't written for a month. I just haven't had the heart. I've been looking carefully into my children's faces, listening carefully to what they say, surrounding myself with good words, prayer, and quiet. Maybe we aren't too late.

This month, Daniel had two big dates with cute girls, took his oath of office to the high school student council, and immersed himself in Spanish cramming for the AP test.

The kids are talking to us more. Daniel lounges in our bedroom visiting. They are all learning to play guitar.

June 10, 1998
Daniel had great experiences at Scout leadership training camp.

September 14, 1998
Yesterday was hard. It was Sunday and Sundays are especially difficult when I happen to be discouraged or distressed about anything. I had planned the night before to skip most of church and just be there long enough to teach my lesson which I had scarcely looked at. I sat in the bathtub with tears flowing down my face like water. Then I thought of President Hinckley (I've just finished reading his biography) and suddenly realized I was immobilized by self-pity. "Forget yourself and go to work." So I

prayed that I'd get a hold of my emotions, sat down, prepared my lesson, and went to church. This felt good, and in my state of mind, I think it was a great triumph.

My worst fear yesterday was not being able to hold back tears. In sacrament meeting something brought them on again but I tried so hard to hold them back that my throat constricted. I thought I would choke it was so painful. But I rallied. I got through my lesson although I don't know if it was any good. Everywhere I looked, I saw people whose problems were like sunbeams compared to the dark, ugly shadows that hung over my mind and shrouded my heart. I was sure my problem was the absolute worst problem anyone could imagine. I still think it is. The only comfort is that Daniel is only one step off the right path. He hasn't traveled very far down the wrong road yet. But his thought patterns seem fixed, his lying and deceiving ingrained.

The reason I am having such a hard time is that we are back to the drawing board with Daniel. Friday morning I discovered evidence that he was back to thinking and doing the things we thought he had promised to quit. I was so sure those things were behind us. We had taken every precaution, we thought. We had worked so hard. It's been a sad weekend. Paul and I are heartbroken. I was so disappointed, I didn't speak directly to Daniel all weekend. On Saturday night he came down with the flu and was throwing up at work. Paul and I went and got him since he has no car privileges but I paid no attention to him. Normally, I would have showered him with care and sympathy and love. But I am so angry and bitter, hurt, afraid, repulsed, and sick.

On Sunday I passed on the sacrament. I felt I was too angry and bitter to partake, and hoped I could soften my heart by next Sunday. This morning I made pancakes with fresh raspberries and apologized to Daniel. It came to me as I made breakfast that whether Daniel overcomes his problem forever, or if he continues to fight it off and on, or whatever happens—even if he gives in—whether I was kind and loving to him, or angry, cold, and closed off to him, may not make any difference to him but it will make a great difference to me, to my spiritual growth and even to my salvation. If I am doing all I can—loving, praying, discussing, teaching, encouraging—then if Daniel chooses to go down the wrong path, it will not be because of anything I did. So I had better rid myself of selfish bitterness, soften my heart toward him, separate the sin from the child of God and work to help him. "Be ye therefore wise as serpents, and harmless as doves." (Matthew 10:16.) I am faced with the challenge to love someone without trusting him for even a minute.

I am so sorry for my darling Daniel. To have a problem like this is such a blight on an otherwise good and wholesome existence. I see now that the pattern of his young life has become one of little deceptions and tiny hidden indulgences. How pitiful is a person with no self-control! He knows things are wrong but goes after them without a second thought! I can't imagine it! No battle. No remorse (until caught). No conscience. I can hardly bear to look at him. His innocent exterior is suddenly transparent and shouts out at me like a blatant lie.

My shoulders curl into my chest. My face is a painful mask. I keep the letter Daniel wrote (the latest one) under my pillow. I don't believe he means what he says but it's my only comfort and hope for the future.

Paul is a brick through all of this nightmare. He won't give up. Most of the time I think it's hopeless and say so. But he refuses to see the worst. He also feels partly responsible because five months ago when he was SURE he erased access to the offensive material on the computer, it turned out he hadn't. I have had a hard time forgiving this mistake—Paul has shed tears, too. I had asked him time and time again if the internet was gone and he repeatedly reassured me that it was. Turned out he had only erased the icon and all Daniel had to do was plug the whole thing back in. Horrors. All the talk of G-rating our home was a sham. How insidious is Satan! Anyway, Paul has taken EVERY precaution this time, and has explained to my satisfaction why he didn't go so far the last time. It's understandable and I am more wary than ever about the creeping, pervasive evil of the internet, computer, machines, technology. I know it can be good, but if it can damage a home like mine, what destruction must it be reaping in less protected places? Is it worth the risk? If a person who just doesn't know quite enough technologically to get rid of it, can't get rid of it, that is too frightening for words. This is what happened to us. It was still connected from the office where Paul uses it for good things but now it's discontinued from the source and he also removed the modem, a piece of machinery from the computer itself, which is what I thought had been done in the first place. However, none of this really matters if Daniel does not ultimately change because he will leave home in the next year or two and will have to insulate himself from evil influences (without our help) for the rest of his life.

I think of what the near future was supposed to bring—Eagle Scout award, seminary graduation, application to BYU, mission preparation—and fear the time is too short and all is LOST. How can a person change so much in so short a time? Paul and Daniel are reading aloud *The Miracle of Forgiveness*.

Like the bishop said, it's a process. We've taken some backward steps but can now go forward if Daniel will. My greatest worry is the thickness of his skull and the hardness of his heart. How can the Spirit reach him? He seems to have no guts, no insides, no heart, no conscience. And yet 99% of the time he outwardly does all the right things. An enigma.

Now I've gone and written too much negative terribleness in my journal.

I've just been reading back in this journal from when we first knew Daniel was in trouble. Maybe we tried to change things too quickly and drastically. The bishop said big drastic changes don't work and don't last. Hmm. So I guess we better go to Disneyworld as planned although the whole idea sounds frivolous and meaningless to me. I have wanted to cancel the whole thing.

President Hinckley says, it's easy to go through the motions but it takes much more effort, time, energy, and thought to really apply gospel principles, to examine the state of your spirit.

I love my son Daniel so much. To imagine that he is lost, that his future happiness is in danger, that his life will be miserable, is more than I can bear. I see, though, that I have to keep loving him no matter what.

Paul called an old missionary companion who is a psychiatrist and described Daniel's behaviors. He was very encouraging and kind and positive, and would like to see Daniel. He said if he has a compulsive, obsessive disorder, he can be "healed." Paul made an appointment for tomorrow. I shed grateful tears that there may be something we can do to help Daniel figure this all out. This doctor uses gospel principles as well as clinical therapy.

I had an interesting experience at a big bookstore. Paul and I went there on an errand for Sam. I was in the children's book section when a salesperson walked right up to me and said, "What's all this?" pointing to my forehead. "Your brow is knitted." Then he told me to follow him, that he knew of a book I should read. He handed me a book *(You are Special* by Max Lucado) and suggested I find a comfortable chair to sit and read it. Right then Paul came up and we sat down and read it. Tears flowed. It was just what we needed, to soften our hearts and reassure us in the middle of our worries, to remind us how important each child of God is, including me and Paul. Including Daniel.

September 16, 1998
Paul and I took Daniel to see Dr. Crandall. It was just a getting-acquainted thing and Daniel has agreed to go back to figure out why his actions are so contradictory to his personality and beliefs. Daniel was shocked for a moment that we were taking what seemed such a drastic step—he didn't think he was so "sick" and wept as we got in the car after the session. We reassured him that he isn't sick, but maybe this counseling will help in some way. What potential this boy has! Dr. Crandall. told Paul there may be something under a few layers that Daniel doesn't

realize that is causing him to act out in disobedient, bizarre, compulsive ways. I am filled with relief and gratitude that there is some help available and that it is gospel-oriented. Daniel seems lighter and happier already. There is hope. The whole thing is that Daniel wants to do right but something prompts him against his judgment to act out. I'm reading a book Dr. Crandall loaned me about obsessive-compulsive disorder, which I don't think Daniel has, though he may have OCPD, a less severe problem. I am learning a lot about myself in this book, too. I have been plagued at times with negative thoughts that won't go away. The book is fascinating and enlightening—on how to rid yourself of destructive thoughts and behavior.

November 8, 1998

I haven't written for so long there was a layer of dust on this journal! We've been so busy with marching band competitions, meetings, bus trips. As the drum major, Daniel has had to put up with a lot. The program is disorganized, the other drum major and several band members quit, plus a jealous band member who was sure she would make drum major is spreading lies about him. He has been discouraged at times but hung in there. Come to think of it, it has been a test of character and he has come through with flying colors. He forgave this girl and went forward as best he could, putting all his energy and love into it. A good boy. He has been better. Passing the Spanish AP test, being on the student council, enjoying his new job at the video store, all these things have helped build confidence and shifted his attention and kept him busy. He loves the music they're doing in choir, he loves clogging, and he is still practicing his drawing constantly. His countenance is open and loving toward us, and he acts like his same old silly and obnoxious self. He did the funniest thing with his old plastic shark-on-a-stick. We laughed so hard—my face was wet with tears. He used the shark like a puppet and had it sing "Oh, Holy Night" with feeling and vibrato. Too silly. Guess you had to be there.

January 11, 1999
The moral state of our country is so depressing. This awful scandal at the White House and subsequent impeachment of our president is a horrible disappointment. And even worse is the scheming, stalling, and lying. Like President Hinckley said on TV, this president has fractured our country.

January 24, 1999
I have been storing up in my mind things I am grateful for. Here is my list:

☐ Daniel getting his Eagle Scout Award.
☐ Daniel getting his BYU application done.
☐ Daniel's very tight hug after he looked at me and said, "Mom, don't you think I'm doing better?"

Yes. Yes. Yes. He is doing better. I should tell him every day. We talked about integrity and he said he's so relieved and happy to be worthy of what people think of him, to be acting in accordance with his beliefs and what he knows to be right.

Part III

my darling from the lions

May 3, 1999

This is the perfect time to take the trip of a lifetime. I am planning to tag along with Daniel's clogging group to Europe to perform at folk dancing festivals. Three-and-a-half weeks! I am going to the library for some French language tapes. I am up for this!

The house was full and noisy Sunday evening for hours as we celebrated Paige's birthday. Laughing, singing, talking, guitar playing, tetherball tournament outside in the yard, tickling, teasing, eating. It was noisy but Paul and I just let it ring!

I'm grateful Daniel came home tonight for a little while in the middle of scout leadership camp. He took a shower, got dressed up and went to his interview at the stake president's office to become an elder. He smelled like a campfire. Thank you, Heavenly Father.

So grateful for the temple. Paul and I have been going every Wednesday at 5 P.M. I so look forward to it and enjoy the peace and opportunity to feel grateful. I do what the temple president told us to do. I ask Heavenly Father to consecrate the time and effort I am spending in the temple to the welfare of my children.

June 1, 1999
I figured out the reason I sometimes feel miserable. I enjoy it—
or I want to be miserable because it is easier than forgiving
myself and having enough faith in God's plan and the Atonement.
This was a revelation to me. It is harder to exercise faith than to
be miserable. No wonder I often give in to misery, wallowing in
my mistakes—my own or others'—dwelling on disappointments,
fretting about the future, expecting the worst, looking at the
dark side. Instead, I could lean toward the light, concentrate on
hope—a vague sort of hoping for good things to come. How
about this: hope, but not for specifics. Hope for long-range
happy endings.

That's what's often missing in my life. I tend toward the tragic.

The best kind of hope is the hope for eternal life.

August 20, 1999
It's been a wonderful trip to Europe with the cloggers but all I
can think of is that in three days I'll be home. Whenever I see
Daniel we give each other big hugs and walk arm-in-arm. (We
are staying with different families in their homes so I don't see
him much.)

September 26, 1999
Today I am grateful for the country I live in and call home.
What a feeling of abundance, opportunity, and energy is ours!

I'm so grateful for the Church. My awareness has been sharpened, my convictions strengthened, my focus narrowed. All through the meeting* last night I wanted to say Yes! Yes! Yes! The Church is true and led by the Lord. This is a call to arms. It's time to do what needs to be done, to step up, to make a difference, to speak out, to use our energy in meaningful ways, to strengthen our homes, marriages and families, to get back to basics. There is too much at stake.

September 27, 1999
Another mini-crisis. Funny, I could feel it coming. Daniel needs our help. He needs some depth, some conviction. I need to study up on his problems. Maybe his little trials are to strengthen him, maybe he's going to need a lot of faith. There is no time to let up. What a lot of good qualities he has. He is a diamond in the rough. His temptations will serve some purpose. I'm just so grateful he didn't do worse things and that we can talk to him and he is not past feeling but full of them—conflicting, uninformed, and unhealthy though they may be!

September 28, 1999
Daniel came home all excited about the Sibelius hymn he is singing for conference with the Men's Chorus. I'm so thankful he is having a good experience at BYU. He wrote me a sweet email about how he is really getting into the Book of Mormon.

October 5, 1999
I am still living on the wonderful evening a week ago. We went to Natalie and Daniel's combined chorus concert at BYU and

---

*Refers to LDS General Women's Conference, September 25, 1999.

then out to Brick Oven for a late supper. All the kids were happy and animated and bright and funny.

I loved every minute of General Conference and was sad it had to end. I'm grateful for my new calling as a Relief Society counselor and feel it is important, that I can perhaps make a contribution and be of some service—at least I pray I can.

January 10, 2000
The bishop said, There is much we don't know, but oh, what we do know: God loves us.

Will the truth hit us in the face when we die? The truth about everything? All our mistakes? All our wrong thinking? All our pride and offenses?

I am reading *I Capture the Castle* by Dodi Smith. "Cruel blows of fate call for extreme kindness in the family circle."

March 27, 2000
The last years have been hard. I thought Daniel's problems would do me in. I haven't coped well most of the time. I felt sorry for myself, vented too much on others, sank into doubt, fear, depression, and negativity. I have been lost. As I have struggled to get a grip, I found lots of tips and quotations and advice and scriptures and truths, but I didn't act on anything with any consistency. Now I am in a clearing. Daniel seems to be out of the woods and got his mission call to Mexico.

I envision a whole new me. I have to be a whole new me. If I don't I'll become ill in some way, sick with fear and worry and wishing things were different. It's time to regain my balance—which I've never had much of all my life, I think—just glimpses. I'm really going to work on it now.

Despite my shortcomings, the Lord has been blessing me with spiritual reassurances. We have been going to the temple on Saturday mornings early. One of those mornings after the 6:30 A.M. session, I walked into the celestial room and the sun coming through the tall window on the east wall was so white and bright I had to shield my eyes. But I wanted to look at it, to bathe in it even though it made my eyes water. The sun was so bright that the light of the huge chandelier looked yellow and soft compared to it. My life has been so dark lately, so full of worry. I wanted to let the light sink into my skin and make me full of light again. Was this the brightness Joseph Smith saw in the First Vision? It was glorious.

We watched *The Wizard of Oz* with the grandkids—they had never seen it. I love the words of the song they sing after the snow falls and cures them of the poison poppies. There they were, their progress stopped, giving up, and then a miracle. This is what I've hoped for during this long period of trouble we've had. "You're out of the woods, you're out of the dark, you're out of the night. Step into the sun, step into the light." Daniel came up to me one morning and reassured me that everything was better now and quoted those words. I still wonder and worry for him, but he is on the right path now at last. It was just a process and I tried to rush it but you can't force people to change. Like my friend Nina says, "You just increase your prayers."

March 29, 2000
Today was a laidback day. I did my exercises, I sewed a little, cleaned some kitchen cupboards, Lindsay came over, I cuddled Lacy and hugged Logan, made a nice dinner with lots of colorful vegetables, sat around with the kids, talked to Mom on the phone, watched *A Goofy Movie* with Daniel while Paul worked on the computer, Daniel's best friend Jake came over and he and Daniel visited with me until late. When I was in bed, Daniel came in to kiss me goodnight as always and again reassured me he is doing well and not to worry. I fell asleep with his whispered words in my ear.

March 30, 2000
I think I've always tried to do too much. I'm feeling like there might be another kind of life to live that I might enjoy more, without guilt, without pressures of my own making. I feel on the verge of some realizations about myself, a gradual dawning of some basic truth that will set me free and strengthen my soul and ground my frenetic thoughts. Maybe I'm finding out how to like myself without any reasons, aside from any accomplishments, just because I am a person. Why couldn't I have known this all my life?

Went to a stake Relief Society leadership meeting. It was great. I'm so thankful to Heavenly Father for making me receptive to what I heard there. A sister from Provo spoke. There were some hard concepts, some challenges, some much-needed depth of understanding. I'm going to copy down the notes I took:

Repentance is a gift, a fresh view, a continual turning of the heart and mind to Christ. Without repentance there can be no progress. It is not optional—it is a commandment. If we aren't feeling the Spirit, we have to repent. Repentance is turning back to God continually, moment by moment. The result will be an outpouring of the Spirit. Read spiritual material with spiritual eyes. If you turn to God continually, you'll know what you're supposed to do. But no, we tend to listen to the wisdom of men instead of turning to God. We listen to men all day long. Pay no attention to that. Stick to the doctrines of Christ—that's what saves. Man's wisdom does not. The Holy Ghost is an individualized instructor. The Spirit accelerates learning. Ask Heavenly Father who you are, then remember it and teach it. If you happen to receive the praise of men, pay it no mind. Lay it gratefully at Heavenly Father's throne and keep working.

I had been praying to know what to do to make some changes. Now I know. It is this gospel principle—repentance—that really fixes everything, although it's not easy. It requires a new way of thinking and (sometimes) a new way of doing. The other precept this sister taught was how we should be very aware of adulation. As we teach our lessons, all the glory should go to Heavenly Father. All. I think it's so simple, but difficult to internalize because we are so steeped in the ways of the world.

April 1, 2000
Such a beautiful sunny spring Saturday. In between Conference sessions, I made bread and we had wonderful ham sandwiches. Daniel and Paul went to the priesthood session. Daniel sang with the BYU choirs at the brand-new Conference Center in Salt Lake City.

April 2, 2000
I love conference—I am sad when it ends. It's good to feel this way—hungering to hear spiritual guidance. I haven't always felt this way. Where have I been? I think I have spent my life filled with pride and ingratitude. I've broken through to a new awareness, an open heart, a desire and willingness to improve and find depth and meaning, strength and commitment.

April 3, 2000
Daniel came home late from work wanting to watch a movie with me. The movie looked pretty silly but he insisted and I watched it with him. Then we had a gospel discussion into the night. He is on the right path: repentance and gratitude. I am coming to understand these principles, too.

April 4, 2000
So much is happening in our family I can hardly absorb it all. Two college graduates, two babies coming, one missionary, another wedding! After all I can do, I lay it all at Heavenly Father's feet—the stress and feelings of being overloaded, bad or good things. Because of my Savior I can do this.

April 6, 2000
We went to the stake center to attend the Palmyra Temple dedication via satellite. What a spiritual occasion. We are so blessed by the Lord to live in this day. I feel like President Hinckley who said, "because of the extraordinary significance of this temple, I am almost completely overcome." In Book of Mormon days they fell to the ground overcome with joy at such times. I thought we might have done that today if it had been socially acceptable.

Part IV

Yea, they opened their mouth wide

April 12, 2000
I haven't been able to write for a week. The worst has happened and I didn't even see it coming.

It was after the temple dedication, after we changed out of our Sunday clothes and picked up the routine of our day, that it happened. Daniel was lying on his stomach on the living room couch watching me as I moved around the room straightening things. He said, "Mom." Something in the way he said that one word sent a piercing chill through my shoulders. I knelt beside the couch with my face inches from his. I asked him what was the matter. He said he needed to tell me something that he didn't feel good about. Then he told me. It felt like a train wreck.

Daniel has done some things. Over these last months. Things I can't write. They probably don't let boys go on missions who have done things like this.

The night he confessed I couldn't stay in the house. I left without telling anyone. I walked along the streets and started climbing the mountain. Partway up I slumped down on a rock, turned my face in the direction of home and began to weep. Tears slid down my face and my neck in sheets and soaked my shirt

through to my skin. I spoke out loud to God. I asked Him to
give me anything but this. Please. Anything but this. After a
while I went home, even though it wasn't the home I've always
thought it was. What else was there to do?

I'm calm now. A friend loaned me some tapes to listen to about
applying the gospel*. I've been listening to them constantly—in
the bedroom, in the kitchen, in the yard while I work. I don't
understand it all yet, but it's comforting to hear the words. They
feel true. I see that all my life I haven't handled my problems the
way I could have to get over them better and faster. I have let
them overwhelm and overcome me. To be steadfast means to
see things as Christ sees them, from a spiritual perspective, long-
range. That way, there is much cause for hope and joy through
the day no matter what is happening.

I pray that I will only go forward from this point, that I'll be
patient with myself and not condemn myself for not knowing
what I'm learning—just be grateful for the insight and go with it.

I'm praying for miracles, that I'll remember and apply all the
things I know and am studying so that I can function as a person, wife, and mother, and be happy and enjoy the day. That will
be a miracle to me. Also, that Daniel will internalize all these
things so he can overcome his temptations and be retaught the
true and correct principles. It's so hard and humbling for me to
realize my efforts as his mother were not enough, weak and
ineffectual compared to the world's influence. I'm sure this is the
wrong way to think, but isn't it true? Nevertheless, this is what's
happened.

* *Becoming Spiritually Centered and Overcoming the World* by James B. Cox.

Part IV

Heavenly Father is really blessing me. In the last week so many good things have happened. Also, I think the Lord prepared me for this crisis so that it wasn't even more devastating. Daniel's mission is postponed. He won't be leaving in July as planned.

I'll start at the beginning. But I don't want to go into any details because right now I am feeling good and I don't want to remember all the pain. I'll just say it's been an up and down year-and-a-half, filled with both fears and hopes.

Slowly, through the forward and backward steps, I began to realize that Daniel's problem was worse than we thought. But he wasn't ready to get fixed. My timetable is not the Lord's or Daniel's. I got impatient many times and tried to force things but that didn't work.

There was that one day I approached Daniel, gently suggesting that he might not be ready to leave on his mission, and he crumpled—he just lay there curled in the fetal position on the floor of his room sobbing that he had to go, worrying about what people would think, assuring me he was ready.

There were those times when fear hit me, the fear that things were going to get a lot worse before they got better. And this could still be true today even though it sure seems like we have hit rock bottom.

Anyway, I don't know whether we have hit rock bottom or not. I pray I have had enough adversity to teach me everything I need to know—everything I can possibly learn and apply for the rest of my life so that this is the worst it will get. But, I don't think so. I still feel the grip of fear through my shoulders—whether it's left over from past troubles or a sign that more are to come—I don't really want to know. It's unthinkable that it could get worse. But that's totally beside the point. The point is: this life is a test. Bad things are going to happen now and again, a lot or a little. Now is the time to build up a reservoir of faith, learn to think of all things as spiritual, realize everything that happens is part of THE PLAN, that Heavenly Father knows and will help through His Son. That's the point.

I've had so many little helps. I feel I am being led along like a little lost lamb, the one the Savior loves so much and goes out to find. Everything points to relying on the Lord every minute, doing everything with trust in him, repenting of every selfish, worldly, prideful thought just as they come into my head.

As you see, I am having to work very hard on building my own spiritual strength to be able to cope with Daniel's problems. I was in the valley of despair and I am climbing out, my "spiritual Mt. Sinai," as President Faust calls it. I'm so grateful to have time and quiet and sunshine and a nice place to do it in.

We're doing all we can for Daniel. He is relatively easy to deal with now—at the moment—and takes our suggestions. He is beginning to act on some of the things we say to do and listens to our long talks. He is beginning to make comments and ask questions during our discussions. I think he is pondering things more now. But this is all strangely aside from my own struggle. Only Daniel can make the changes deep within himself to get whole. Only I can make the changes deep within myself to get whole. Our lives don't depend on each other. Only the Lord can help us as individuals. So it doesn't matter if we are at rock bottom or not. What matters is that we learn to turn to the Lord. It mustn't matter if Daniel messes up again and again. Not to me. What matters is if I can lay this burden at Jesus' feet and bear a song away.

That was really hard to write. Sometimes I feel like I'll die if Daniel goes backward and the absolute worst gradually descends on him. It's unthinkable. I saw a program on TV once about a man dying of AIDS and his mother was nursing him at home as he slowly, slowly died. His body was like a skeleton with skin stretched over it, skin covered with big dark sores. I am filled with dread. But I don't think I will be healed or learn what I'm supposed to learn until I give it all up. Give up all my earthly hopes and dreams and turn them over to the Lord. I can't hope that Daniel's wrong ideas will be healed on our time schedule. The counseling we are setting up, the talks we are having, all of these are weak efforts at aiding Daniel. It's worthwhile, yes, but not the answer and not the end. I guess some people are healed through counseling, or a combination of positive efforts. But my hope has to be based on the Lord, that in the very end, if I have put my foundation in Christ (Helaman 5:12) everything will be okay—and not just okay but glorious.

I'm struggling. The fear keeps gripping me through my neck, shoulder, and back. I have no appetite. It's an effort to do the smallest thing. I know this is no good—it is a temporal approach. I must keep working to go forward. Minute by minute. Listen to the tapes, study the scriptures, recall who I am, pray to repent of my weakness and be steadfast, see as Christ sees, try to be grateful, enjoy the day, work around the house, pray about everything.

These things will shield me, protect me with the shield of faith. I must make Heavenly Father and Jesus the center of my life. All day long. (D&C 59:5.)

Maybe this grip of fear is Satan trying to discourage me. Maybe he thinks I will give in. I've got to get rid of the fear and dread. Be not afraid. Only believe.

If my kid's behavior or problem is the most dominant thing in my mind, I need to get the beam out of my eye. God has to be dominant.

I can say and write all of this but oh, is it hard to do it minute by minute. Sleep is the only break—and I mustn't do too much of it. I'm so tired.

I can say, I will endure this for Heavenly Father. And my Savior will help me endure it.

Once each hour, all through the day, I say a prayer. *Father, I am Thy daughter, born in thy courts of glory. I know Thou lovest me with perfect love. Help me to feel Thy love right now, today.* Ten or twelve times a day. Pray. Keep praying.

Time to grow up. Eat. Get up early. Do your daily tasks for Heavenly Father. Turn the fear over to Christ. Enjoy the day. I see now how I've been wrong in the past. I woke up this morning realizing this.

I wonder if I can keep this spiritual perspective up. I know I am going to fail sometimes. I need to get a blessing. The dread keeps coming back and sitting on my shoulders like a vulture. It fills my whole body with an uneasy chilling ache. I can't find a physical way to shake it off. I'm going to try the spiritual route.

This is why I can't afford any distractions right now. Maybe, to keep on the strait and narrow, I can't afford any distractions for the rest of my life. By distractions I mean doing, saying, thinking, watching, reading, participating in anything that I can't feel comfortable doing for Heavenly Father as a stewardship assignment. It strikes me that I am actually on the same level as Daniel. We both have to work on the same things. Sin is sin, I guess. The same principles apply to any level of spiritual darkness, to any level of healing from sin.

Say: *Heavenly Father, Daniel is thy son.* Then, see him dressed in white temple clothes, the robes of the Holy Priesthood. See him being exalted.

I think Darwin's theory of evolution, even if parts of it are true to a degree, is a tool and a creation of Satan to get man to believe there is no God and no right and wrong, that we are animals enslaved by instinct with no ability to reason and choose.

April 16, 2000

I've been discouraged as I've discovered Daniel's problems to be pathological rather than a conscious choice to do evil, thinking it's harder to cure or heal a disease than to change a sinful disposition. Just now it came into my head that it's actually the other way around. In this day and age, if Daniel's heart is in the right place, there is knowledge and therapy and understanding and methods that can cure diseases. It's the intent of a man's heart that's impossible to influence—if his heart is hard. Daniel's heart is soft. I know that. I know him. For that reason, I'm allowing a tiny hope to enter my own heart—that he'll be better—not just in the next life but in this life as well. This is a comforting thought. Thank you, Heavenly Father.

I've been saying that little prayer regularly reminding myself of who I am—a daughter of God who He loves with perfect love. I say this type of thing many times a day. It helps. I feel the Spirit and I'm able to carry on.

April 20, 2000
I had a little breakdown. I see now how it happened. I try too hard to fix things, even myself. I try to be perfect instead of being satisfied with progress. I want everything fixed right now or at least on track. I can't make this happen. I can't control other people. There is too much I don't know. So I tried to know it all and there's no way.

I went to the library and got a book out and read about pornography, why people look at it and what it does to them. It was so sad and ugly and shocking. Then, for weeks we didn't hear back from the bishop about getting help from LDS Family Services so we made our own appointment as best we could. At one of the darkest moments of my life, sitting there in that office, waiting and waiting for our appointment, and then waiting and waiting while Daniel was in there behind that closed door, I looked at my wonderful husband sitting there right next to me and began to imagine that this was somehow his fault, that maybe he abused Daniel when he was little, or some awful thing. Of course I couldn't tell Paul what I was thinking so I just sat there feeling worse and worse. He, my own dear husband, started to look strange to me, like I didn't know a thing about him. Everything around me took on a dark and dirty aspect. I began to think the mouth of hell must be gaping open to swallow me.

And then when Daniel came out and Paul and I went in to talk with the therapist, things got even more bizarre. He seemed so uncaring and matter-of-fact, saying the most frightening things about how nothing could be done for Daniel. After all, he does have some feminine mannerisms, he said, such as a lisp. What was he talking about? It's hardly noticeable. And anyway, what does a physical characteristic have to do with being drawn to look at pornography? Does the way your teeth and your tongue move together make you a homosexual? Not long ago the orthodontist told me Daniel's bite was a little off and could be fixed easily with braces—so how can that have anything to do with his sexuality?

All these things multiplied and got worse and sped up in my head. When we got home I lost it. Really lost it. But not enough to give up entirely. I just couldn't stop crying. I knew I needed help. I even had the presence of mind to remember that it might help to breathe into a paper bag because I was feeling light-headed. What do you know—it worked. I knew that everything that was happening was all too shocking and distressing for me. I should have known sooner. I guess as I was plugging along I was also getting more and more anxious. Paul took me to the doctor who asked me, on a scale of one to ten, how bad my situation was. I said it was a ten. He gave me some little pink pills that are supposed to calm me down for a few weeks and then

I'm supposed to start taking some other pills. He said in a couple of weeks I should be better. I stared at the tiny pill in my hand for a long time. I didn't want to take it. But I finally did. It was such a humbling, terrible thing to feel so helpless . . .

May 3, 2000
I never had to take all those pills. I got a hold of my emotions but I'm still having a hard time turning my problems over to the Lord, at the same time praying and studying to be an instrument in his hands to help Daniel. Here he is, still living at home, and we are still hoping he can go on a mission some time. But I feel like my efforts are for nothing. I'm pouring all my energy into him and it bounces off. When do I give up? But I'm not supposed to give up, ever. Shall I just relax and not try so hard? How do I know when I'm trying too hard or not hard enough? Shall I not try at all? Shall I remove my heart out of my body and place it somewhere else? A heart transplant? Shall I close up shop? It is killing me. I'm dying inside. Maybe I should ponder it a little each day and then let it go for the rest of the time. I can't own Daniel's problem.

I guess I have some good moments, but more bad. I think this is understandable. I've lived a whole life with nothing this horrendous ever happening to me. And now I'm faced with this most horrible thing. I can't expect myself to change overnight into a paragon of spiritual strength. But I am making progress. Daniel has done awful things but I don't have to give him charge of my heart and soul, my goals, my happiness, and my day. He mustn't control me. My job is to be an instrument to help Daniel change. But it can't be my god—it can't dominate me.

Part IV

Paul and I finally had a meeting with Dr. Matthews. This is the new therapist at LDS Family Services who specializes in helping people overcome pornography addiction and homosexuality. It was very enlightening. He said we need to avoid two mistakes: taking Daniel's problem too seriously and not taking it seriously enough. He said that Daniel became vulnerable to homosexuality because he got involved in male pornography. He says he fits the profile of the type of boy who falls into this trap: bright, curious, overconfident. They get hooked by their intense curiosity, saying something like, "I've got to get to the bottom of this." He said that in Daniel's case, internet pornography was the problem, not homosexuality. We need to take the immorality factor more seriously than the fact that it was homosexual. Homosexuality is just sexual energy gone awry.

Dr. Matthews explained it like this. Imagine a perfectly level field. In the middle of the field is a spigot. If you turn on the water, it will make a puddle, but if you plow a furrow, the water will begin to flow in that direction. Daniel's sexual energy was beginning to flow in a healthy channel. Then the same-sex pornography blocked that flow and the water was forced to go in another direction. This is what homosexuality is like. The wayward trench got deep fast. Now Daniel has to direct the flow of the water back into the right furrow. Since Daniel has quit looking at the pornography, it's like the blockage has been removed and the water will get flowing back into its original channel. While this may not be true for all who struggle with homosexuality, it seems to be true in Daniel's case.

Daniel's prognosis for getting straightened out is good because he has a strong history of heterosexual attraction, a good relationship with his father, and an orthodox view of the Church. Dr. Matthews said Daniel listened to and believed all the lessons he was taught in church and at home about being chaste with girls and started exploring sexuality in the male direction. It all happened very, very gradually. He said that for Daniel, the issues of immorality and dishonesty are currently more serious than the homosexual issue.

We are not to toss out all the good things Daniel has done. They were perfectly sincere and legitimate. But a lot of his spirituality so far has only been conformity. He said Daniel needs to suffer some—he can learn from suffering. He has been overconfident, naive and immature. What happened to Daniel is mostly due to the stupidity of his youth.

Daniel told me Dr. Matthews said that changing how he has been thinking is like saying "Rudolph the red-nosed—" and not thinking "reindeer." This sounds difficult, but possible. Sometimes, people even replace "reindeer" with something else, like "buffalo." But once in a while, "reindeer" may pop back in there, but it doesn't need to mean anything. Daniel is going to learn how to respond and not to overinterpret these thoughts. Daniel can live an honest, open, and congruent life. He needs to go on his mission and he'll probably do fine there. It's after the mission that is the dangerous time. He said boys can't go on a mission at all if they have been homosexually active unless there is clear evidence of complete and thorough repentance.

So last night I got discouraged. But I don't need to condemn myself. I need to learn from it. My weakness will not help Daniel. But there's a fine line there. Dr. Matthews told us not to coddle him. We have to be stern. I have to learn to be realistic and firm and stay on task helping Daniel and demanding specific accountability, at the same time not letting it get in the way of my regular life. We have to talk with him every day. Did you pray today? What did you pray about? What exactly were your thoughts centered on today? What did you think about while you traveled, worked, talked with others? Did you have any sexual thoughts and fantasies?

We have been having a special prayer together every night, just the three of us. Daniel is in charge of this prayer.

Daniel told me that the secret pornography and homosexuality part of his life had nothing to do with his regular outward life. Dr. Matthews said this compartmentalization is common. People with sexual addictions live double lives all the time. Daniel says he didn't let them cross over. He never had homosexual thoughts about his regular friends. This was a dark, dark side of his life.

Homosexuality isn't always about relationships, it's often just about sexual gratification. The foundation of their interaction is sex. Otherwise, they'd just be friends. Daniel and I talk about how when you see an attractive person of either sex, you shouldn't sexualize them. They're just beautiful or handsome, that's all. We can appreciate that, but the rest is none of our business.

Daniel is learning that his thinking has been all wrong. He's seeing that these thoughts he's held in his head are lies that need not be permanent fixtures in his mind. He can change the way he thinks. He is recognizing that his thoughts were distorted.

This is the same as any other obsession or addiction.

We understand now that Daniel had normal heterosexual feelings that got warped by the pornography, by stereotypes, by the persuasive chat room conversations. His sexual feelings were stimulated and this made him think he was homosexual. But it was just sexual feelings that went off in the wrong direction. Dr. Matthews says there can come a time when Daniel's confused thoughts can be replaced with normal, healthy thoughts.

Heavenly Father, help me to see Daniel's great worth separate from what he does or has done.

I need to change my paradigm. It's not about hope so much as growth. Daniel may never change. It's up to him. My job is to do my part and that's all. Pray to know what I can do to help, pray to increase my spiritual strength, get on with my life. Daniel has us right where he wants us, I guess, though unconsciously. We have to dump this back on him, emotionally. Like Dr. Matthews said, let him suffer. But don't cause him suffering—that doesn't do any good. If he sees me miserable, it puts him in control over me. It makes him in charge. Daniel has to see me being in charge of myself so he will learn to be in charge of himself.

This is so difficult. I see now that I have been giving my agency away all my life—or at least some of it.

This?
I am controlled by others.
I lack confidence.
I am powerless.

I feel worthless.
I'm upset most of the time.
I am dependent on others for my peace and happiness.
I am tossed to and fro.

Or this?
I'm able to love others (and myself).
I'm able to help others.
I feel closer to Heavenly Father.
I have great hope for eternal life.
I feel peace.
I laugh at my humanness a lot.
I feel of greater worth.
I am growing spiritually.
I feel the power of the Holy Ghost.

How to take back my agency: realize the beam is in my own eye,
recognize when I am getting hooked by my kid or allowing him
to upset me, which takes away my freedom, focus spiritually,
repent, get personal revelation. Don't preach at Daniel, just testify, promise, tell him you know a way to get well, whenever he is
ready. Be as clay in the master's hands.

What do I say to people who are asking me when Daniel is leaving on his mission? I can't say what is really happening, but I
don't want to lie. Possible answers:

We don't have a date yet.
Not for a few months.
When he's good and ready.
Not for a while yet.

Daniel comes in and talks to me every night. (Paul tries to stay awake but always ends up snoring.) The pornography filled his mind with lies about his body and sexuality in general. Any kind of pornography does this. So we are undoing these wrong ideas about sex, slowly and surely. We talk a lot about why God gave us sexual feelings and what sex is for and how proper, healthy, normal sexuality is wonderfully pleasurable, unselfish, and loving. We talk about how sexual intimacy is connected with the overall complex, loving, committed relationship between a husband and wife.

I can't believe this happened to my boy. He never missed a day of scripture reading in seminary. He got a big award for it. And what good did all that scripture reading do?

I love the story about President Joseph F. Smith when he had the dream of meeting his uncle Joseph Smith in heaven. He notices his clothes are dirty and has to change them before he stands before the prophet. When he finally gets there, his uncle tells him he is late. Joseph says, "Yes, but I'm clean." I found a copy of the story for Daniel and he loves it. We're not after perfection in this life. We're after being clean and forgiven. Through Christ.

Dr. Matthews calls Daniel's situation a textbook pornography case. I'm making Daniel (and me) a sort of equation to understand what has happened.

>   dissatisfied with body, peer rejection, discouragement
> \+   internet pornography
> \+   overconfidence and curiosity
> \+   lies and deceit
> =   disaster, spiritual darkness, immorality

So the opposite could be:

    self worth as a given apart from anything in this world
+   activities of value such as constant prayer, scripture study, gospel discussions, good books
+   humility, teachableness, repentance, loving self and others, honesty
=   spiritual growth, steadfastness in Christ, ability to grow and deal with life problems, mission, temple, temple marriage, family, eternal life

Daniel and I talked about what to do when a thought pops in his mind that he doesn't want there anymore. We decided we can't help what thoughts pop in our minds. But we can help where it goes from there. We can decide what to do with it—dwell on it or send it away. We can start praying. And if we keep sending bad thoughts away, they will eventually quit coming altogether. Oh, maybe an old thought will pop up once in a while, but it will have no power. We'll know it for what it is: a lie.

They've reorganized the wards in our stake. I've been called to be the Relief Society president of a brand new ward. As I begin, I see that I myself have to start at the beginning—or I'll completely fall apart. Simple as that. In order to get centered and be enabled to dig in with the work I have to remember who I am—a beloved spirit daughter of a glorious Heavenly Father. I am a child of a perfect Father who has a perfect love for me. He knows everything about me, He wants me here, He has given me opportunities to grow. I'm grateful for all these challenges. I have a desire and willingness to develop abilities regarding this particular calling that I do not now possess. I see that I must apply the first principle of the gospel—including faith in the Lord Jesus Christ, whether I need his grace to help me through periods of doubt and anxiety regarding this new calling, or to carry my heavier burdens (Daniel). Large or small, my Savior can fill in the gaps and help me progress.

The officiator saying the prayer in the temple the other day asked that those on the prayer roles would be blessed according to their willingness and righteous desires. This is Daniel. This is me. What if all I have is a righteous desire? No skills, no great understanding, no ability? Just a desire to do right, to serve, to be good, to be holy? This desire is all Daniel has right now, and me, too, in this big church calling. I so appreciated that prayer.

No matter where we are on the strait and narrow, we're where we are supposed to be if we are moving forward. Take comfort in this. Calm yourself. Feel peace. Pray continually.

Why am I here, Lord? I feel totally out of place, leadershipwise.

May 12, 2000
I didn't know this before: I was straying from the strait and narrow when I gave in to fear and discouragement. When you're in the middle of it, it's so difficult to see that, and get back on the path. But once you do it, it gets easier each time. It seems that way lately anyway. Or do I feel this way just because things seem to be going better? I hope I have learned the skills now to make it through hard times better. I hope I've developed some spiritual depth and refinement, so when the fiery darts come I will have my armor in place. It takes constant vigilance. Can't get complacent. Can't let pride in. Have to keep my thoughts pure and spiritually centered.

I love this new way of living. I love knowing how to rely on the Lord. I love this love I feel from Heavenly Father and my Savior. I think I love myself at last.

June 6, 2000
Thank you, Heavenly Father, for a friend like Jake for Daniel. He just shared his testimony with me and explained why he knew he could love Daniel no matter what he did. (Jake doesn't know why Daniel's mission is cancelled.) He has seen a change of heart in Daniel. Elder Oaks said the greatest miracle of all is the mighty change of heart.

But more time has to pass, at least it would seem so. Only two months today since he confessed everything. And it was only a few weeks before, that he did the wrong things that so few people know of. They are too awful to think about.* I don't let myself imagine any of it. I can't. This is my darling boy we are talking about.

Nevertheless, miracles happen and it's up to the bishop and stake president, with the help of Dr. Matthews, and nobody seems to be in much of a hurry about the mission. Including me. I don't want him to go on his mission unless he's all well and it's right.

June 8, 2000
Repentance is evidenced by 1. godly sorrow, 2. confession, 3. sufficient time elapsing to permit a period of probation.

---

*Daniel was persuaded through internet chat rooms to meet with three different men on three different occasions. These men were all returned missionaries. Two were currently temple-married. Although they touched him, it could have been worse.

June 9, 2000

We know our children will make wrong choices to some degree or another because we're all human and are here on Earth to learn. We learn by exercising our agency and suffering consequences and repenting. But there's no guarantee that our children will correct or learn from their bad choices. If they do, whether sooner or later, this is an extra bonus from Heavenly Father. If I as a parent remain steadfast in Christ, in the light, seeking personal revelation on how to help my child as a stewardship assignment, I can grow spiritually no matter what happens, and this is why I am here on Earth. There may be sorrow, there may be great joy. But the emphasis is on my spiritual growth.

I am trying to understand why people have homosexual tendencies. Is this a physical birth defect? Or a medical problem? Is it a spiritual self-worth problem? Is it a problem caused by the world's misguided belief systems? Is it an emotional problem caused by damage in my son's early youth? Is it a mental illness like schizophrenia? Or obsessive-compulsive disorder? Is it the result of sexual abuse? Is it an addiction? Is the addiction caused by mental illness or is the mental illness caused by the addiction? Is the sexual addiction the mental illness or did he have a mental illness before it? Or a susceptibility to it?

If so, Daniel is one or more of these: confused, sick, addicted, schizophrenic, handicapped, blocked, vain, narcissistic, influenced, brainwashed.

He is also full of life, exuberant, talented, a beloved son of Heavenly Father, sensitive, affectionate, loving, gifted, happy.

Can he use these positive things to conquer the negative things? Or will the negative things kill all the others?

I see that Daniel fits the stereotype of what much of society now immediately labels as gay. He is musical, artistic, enthusiastic, more interested in the arts than sports. He was persecuted because of having these good qualities by his peers all his young life. Now I see that if you are cruelly teased, taunted, labeled, and beat up physically and emotionally just for being yourself, the attention, however negative, can tend to make you defensive and distort your thoughts.

I heard or read that for some reason if people are forced to change their behavior, it is only cemented. That's why electric shock therapy doesn't work. I'm so glad we're not trying that kind of method. It sounds so horrible. I can't believe they do it to people.

It also does not work well to try to force something out of our minds by sheer will power, because we are actually reinforcing the thoughts by dwelling on them. Rather than dwell on the negative thoughts, we have to replace them with truth, faith, hope, God's love.

If Daniel lived on a desert island with only loving, accepting people and influences, he would not have these misconceptions and self-destructive behaviors. Daniel's image of himself was molded and maimed by other people and the world. He was ridiculed just for being his bright, enthusiastic self. His compulsive behaviors, from harmless to harmful, would not exist—or would they? What about before the ridicule? As a little child,

Daniel was, on the one hand, delightful, lovable, adorable and on the other hand, volatile, prone to violent tantrums, obsessive about details like tucking his shirt in and the amount of milk in his cup. I think he was born with this difficult nature. So, on the desert island what would have come of this? Is his problem medical? Is it physical? If so, it's so cruel to try to change him in his mind and spirit. He has to want to change.

Pornography doesn't say, "Let's be friends." It has no bearing on reality or relationships and can cause all kinds of wrong ideas and acting out. And it has all kinds of spiritually destructive repercussions. With porn, you get sexual gratification but there is no emotional risk. It's used as an escape, like alcoholism. I think pornography is sexual abuse because it is giving people warped ideas. It abuses sex.

I think pornography is much more evil and powerful than most people know.

Daniel said he thought looking at bad pictures of guys wasn't bad because he had already seen it all—he is one. He was sure that looking at girls would be bad, though. What a strange rationalization. Now that I think about it, he knew in his heart there was something wrong with it because when I caught him unawares he attempted to hide what he was doing and acted guilty and furtive. Were those the times when he was so difficult to live with and would never get off the computer? I didn't see what was happening. Still, the Spirit told him it was wrong, even at the relatively innocent beginning. What made Daniel, as opposed to someone else, keep doing this bad thing? Is it this wicked world? Was it an obsessive, compulsive trait? Was it his pain inside from peer cruelty that made him seek out something he thought might fix it? How horrible to be a boy and yet be told over and over that you aren't a boy, or not the right kind of boy.

I'm remembering one incident in particular. It happened at Mutual around Christmastime. Daniel must have been about 14. The boys in his group all brought white elephant gifts for a gift exchange. They sat in a big circle choosing presents from a pile in the center. When it was Daniel's turn he picked out a nicely wrapped box and opened it to find an old, used, yellowed jock strap. Of course everyone laughed, but Daniel himself became the brunt of the jokes. They told him he of all people sure wouldn't need this gift, that he didn't have the equipment for it. Even two of his friends joined in. And the leaders didn't do or say a thing. Daniel came home and told us about it, sobbing his eyes out. Paul and I went straight over to the chapel and had a talk with the Young Men leaders. They were sorry. They just didn't realize the harm.

Later, the mother of the boy who brought the jock strap called me and apologized. Too late. The damage had been done.

The thing is, this wasn't an isolated incident. Several boys at church teased him relentlessly.

At one point the bishop actually excused Daniel from coming to meetings, which I thought was strange. Why ostracize the picked-on boy? Why not just teach the other kids to be nice? Daniel went to his meetings anyway.

I think it makes sense that all Daniel's problem is caused by his wrong perception of his worth, which is a result of a series of unfortunate incidents in his early youth and through adolescence, the biggest one being the birth of the internet. I keep thinking about how Dr. Matthews said that in Daniel's case, if there were no internet porn, Daniel would not have had homosexual tendencies.

It has nothing to do with so-called feminine traits or personality—only the world's reaction or presumptions or judgments about a person's traits and personality, which reaction was demeaning, damaging and unfairly redefining in Daniel's case. This judgment caused a perfectly nice and wonderful boy to become dissatisfied with himself. It crushed his identity and reformed it into what he thought was the only way he could survive. If Daniel had lived in some other century, his best qualities would have been considered refined and gentlemanly.

There are clues everywhere as to why this happened to Daniel.

Daniel said that in the chat rooms they say to each other that if you are ugly or fat, etc., you are not wanted. So homosexuality is a private club? Is this why Daniel quit eating? He lost about fifteen pounds during his first year at BYU which was during the time he was using the internet to explore homosexuality. They make sure everybody's attractive. Is this the sense of belonging in his own gender that Daniel missed to some degree and longed for? I heard or read somewhere that a general acceptance by one's own gender is really important to healthy emotional development.

I remember when Daniel suddenly started caring about his clothes and appearance more than in the past. Is my nose big? he asked. Does this outfit look good? He wanted to be attractive, even in a twisted way, to his own gender—but only those in this specific group. As far as we can tell, he doesn't think along these lines about anyone else outside this group, such as his best friend Jake.

The pornography started with muscle men pictures and became more graphic from those, including written pornography. He got addicted to the stimulation and kept wanting more. Every addiction is like this. Dr. Matthews said that males, especially in adolescence, can get turned on by practically anything, a thought, a breeze, an image, even nothing.

Daniel was lured by people with whom he had no emotional attachment or relationship. We realized that Daniel began his acting out immediately after Megan, the girl he loved so much, got engaged to some guy Daniel never even heard of. He said it was the worst thing that ever happened to him.

This rejection could have set off a return to the pornography, chat rooms and subsequent meetings, these self-destructive, escapish, desperate attempts for any kind of "acceptance," or comfort or whatever. It seems as if his feelings for Megan and his homosexual tendencies are connected.

I remember how Daniel was head-over-heels in love with this girl for three years during which she treated him pretty badly. On again, off again, allowing other boys in the picture and using Daniel to vent all her boy troubles to, all the while he is in love with her himself. She used him, manipulated him, leaned on him, cried on him, to keep him as her best friend. As time went on his feelings of self-worth were so worn down he began to accept that a platonic friendship was all he could expect from her, or from any girl, and that girls in general did not find him attractive. Even though he eventually gave up on her as a girl-friend, he was still in love with her.

Oh, I wish they never met. I can see why he loved her. She is strikingly beautiful, slender and petite, with a perfect ivory complexion and long perfectly straight shining brown hair. I don't know for sure why she strung him along so cruelly. Her lack of respect for him as a person must have done damage. Because of her own insecurities, and Daniel's also, the relationship went on and on and harmed Daniel immensely—much more than we thought. A graph recording the pattern of his three instances of immoral behavior would follow the exact same lines as his emotional crises surrounding Megan.

*Hopeful signs of Daniel's spiritual growth:

He identified and verbally corrected wrong belief systems. This was an assignment from Dr. Matthews.

He wrote a beautiful, spiritually mature letter to Megan telling her kindly that he wouldn't have anything more to do with her. He commented that it was the most thought he had ever put into an email.

He is showing signs of deep remorse, reaching beyond a temporal perspective.

---

*This is a list from the back of a journal, the entries undated.

He has a special prayer concerning overcoming his problems with his dad and me every night.

He marks off his calendar with an X every day he doesn't do anything bad. He has done this since April 6, the day he confessed two months ago. There is an X on every single day.

Every night he gives us an accounting of his day, his thoughts and his temptations. He told us about a bad dream and how he realized it didn't mean anything.

He is cheerful and helpful! His countenance has changed, gradually but surely.

He is more patient with me and realizes he has to earn back my trust.

He faithfully goes to his appointments with the bishop and Dr. Matthews.

He loves teaching his new Primary class.

He told me how simple and beautiful the Primary lessons are and how he wishes the kids would listen and know what the gospel really means.

Paul reported to me that Daniel voluntarily bore his testimony at the Fathers and Sons camp out.

He is feeling the consequences of his actions and seems fired up to do whatever he has to do to make amends.

He said to me, "Mom, all I want to do is serve the Lord."

He seems more kind, less critical of others.

He spends hours at the piano, playing hymns and Primary songs.

He cares less about what the world thinks and more about what Heavenly Father and his Savior think. We have discussed what godly sorrow is.

He prepared and gave a talk on baptism at two of his Primary kids' baptisms. He was really happy about this.

He is waiting eagerly but patiently for this informal probation to be completely removed. He is so excited to be able to take the sacrament again. He has missed it so much.

He gets up for family devotionals now.

He is reading a book about putting on the armor of the Lord.

He bought missionary journals and started writing in the first one on the day he was supposed to enter the MTC. This particular day was especially difficult and he chose to grow from it and press forward.

He is feeling the painful consequences of his actions.

He now realizes that part of repentance is the time that has to elapse. Soon, he is supposed to call the stake president for an appointment to find out about the status of his mission call. But he says, "I'm not getting my hopes up."

Part IV

June 16, 2000

Meanings in the scriptures have begun to leap out at me, enlightening my mind. I am finally understanding basic gospel principles that had eluded me all my life. I'm so grateful I still have time to apply them. Each day is a gift, a chance to make the Savior's Atonement work in my life and feel Heavenly Father's love. After many years of condemning myself and feeling hopeless, depressed, and tossed to and fro, I am spiritually reborn. I am no longer oppressed with doubts and fears and past mistakes. Every weakness and mistake is taken up by Christ. If I "deny myself of all ungodliness" such as despair, self-loathing, feelings of inadequacy, discouragement, etc., his grace is sufficient. I can be lifted, feel good about myself and others and hope for a joyous eternal life. He heals me.

The words I just wrote are words I have heard all my life, and to someone else they surely must sound trite. I testify that the things I am writing come from deep inside me. I have chosen each word thoughtfully. But there are no adequate words, and not enough of them, to describe what has happened to me in the last two months. I always wondered how to do what King Lamoni's father wished—"Wilt thou make thyself known unto me, and I will give away all my sins to know thee." (Alma 22:18.) I gave away my temporal expectations, my disappointment, my perfectionism, and now I try to turn to Heavenly Father in everything I do. I try to do all my tasks out of love for Heavenly Father and my Savior.

Because of this, my life has changed. I have energy. I find it easier to love others. I want to get to know people and serve them. Life isn't so hard. My burdens feel light. (Mosiah 7.) And every time I get tempted to go back to my old habits I remember who I am, why I am here, and where I am headed. I say a prayer affirming that I am a daughter of God who loves me perfectly despite my blunders and that my Savior loves me too and fills in all my blank spots. Then I press forward—I don't relive my mistakes. I am learning what it means to be steadfast in Christ, to be like him. It's amazing to me that I find myself on the same path as Daniel.

Nothing everlastingly bad ever happens to anyone. Every terrible and hard thing is a chance to turn to Heavenly Father, an opportunity to think, see, feel, and do as the Spirit of the Lord directs, a learning experience, a time to try your faith, a refining fire, a reawakening.

We all have in us the divine characteristic of striving for perfection. Sometimes we just forget we aren't perfect YET and that Heavenly Father loves us anyway right where we are, so much that He provided a rescuer for us to keep us pressing forward with encouragement and hope. We can have our dream of perfection even now, but only in Christ. This is a blessed relief and a joy. I'm striving and whole and I'm going to be perfect someday. Not in this life, but in the next because of Christ.

I am having more spiritual insights and experiences than I can write down.

Sometimes, in this period of newfound peace and depth and joy of life, I hear a voice telling me it won't last, that at some future time I'll look back on this and decide I was a little crazy or fanatical. Or I wonder if something worse than ever will happen and I'll slip back into disbelief and survival mode; my faith won't be strong enough. I know all this is Satan trying to pull me into that awful darkness. It is going to require constant diligence to stay in the light. Thought by thought.

I almost wish I could go home now at this happy time. But there is more to learn and now is the time, the best time, to learn it. They say we learn so much faster on this earth with our bodies. I'm grateful to get more time. I'm so glad I finally started learning. I pray for powers equal to the tasks ahead. I'm not so afraid of life as I used to be. I used to spend a lot of time consumed with little fears.

June 19, 2000
We had all our family here for Father's Day. Noisy, silly, fun. I made my once-a-year fried chicken menu and enjoyed the cheerful, popping, sizzling sounds from the stove. Daniel was down—he's had a hard week. Talking with him, I see he needs to go back to step one: see himself as Christ sees him—a beloved son of a glorious Father in Heaven, and learn to get his feelings of self-worth from that fact only. I urged him to work on this thought through prayer. He said he would. I've done it and I know it works.

June 24, 2000
I think I am no longer condemning myself first thing in the morning and whenever I make a mistake, forget something, or don't measure up to perfection. Instead I ask, "What can I do, Heavenly Father, to serve Thee today?" And with love of God and Jesus in my heart, I press forward. It makes all the difference. Sometimes I want to shout it out: I'm getting it at last! My

understanding is increasing. The truth falls on me like a drench-ing, cleansing rain when I read or hear it. I have purpose in my life—a long-range but real hope. It is real. It's something to strive for. It's a sure foundation. It's everything they said it is. It is the love of God and the Atonement of our Savior. It works if we put forth the least effort. It works for everything.

One thing I have to watch for is thinking I get it all and know it all, just because I am so happy and enthusiastic about the progress that has occurred. I know I've only just begun. There will be more lessons. So much to learn.

I think I am learning to submit to the will of the Lord. Now I've got to get the submitting cheerfully part down. (Mosiah 24:15.)

"Christ knows better than all others that the trials of life can be very deep and we are not shallow people if we struggle with them." (Elder Holland, Nov. 1999 Ensign.)

How do I know if I am faithful? Can the word *faithful* really and truly just mean full of faith? I think I can know I am faithful if I feel the Spirit. And I can't feel the Spirit if I am in despair, upset, confused, worried, dissatisfied. I have to accept what's happening in my life as Heavenly Father's will and rely on my Savior. Then work and pray and live because I love God and Christ.

"I will not leave you comfortless: I will come to you." (John 14:18.)

"The Church is concerned primarily with worship of the Lord Jesus Christ. Our great mission is to testify of his living reality. We should not be involved in anything not in harmony with his major objective. We should be involved with whatever is in harmony with this objective." (Pres. Hinckley, p. 52, Nov. 1999 Ensign.)

June 29, 2000

I haven't done so well the last few days. Many of my former fears have returned and I can't remember how to think so they'll go away. The condemning of myself came back, along with the knowledge of my inadequacies. I've been fearing the worst for Daniel and hating my Relief Society job. I am not being steadfast. I am so missing feeling the Spirit. I cry a lot. I'm not happy, I was so wishing I could have that Spirit for the rest of my life. It was so wonderful loving myself for the first time ever. I got so much done. I enjoyed my life so much more. I'm trying to get refocused but it doesn't come back. It's like one minute I am filled with God's love for myself and everyone else and the next minute it's gone. I was being held up by something and it disappeared. I guess I go back to step one. I am a beloved spirit daughter of God. My life has meaning and purpose and direction. I am devoted to Jesus Christ, my Savior and Exemplar. I am a woman of faith . . .

I have such a long way to go. I need my every word and thought directed, every blunder forgiven, every small effort aimed. It's back to praying every hour. I need Thee every hour.

July 5, 2000

I've been so disappointed. I'm trying to figure out what caused that wonderful Spirit I had enjoyed for several weeks to leave. I think I wasn't valiant enough. I began the negative thoughts. It takes such perfect diligence and I am not perfect. I mustn't condemn myself for this bad week, these dark hours, these doubts. That doesn't do any good. I guess it's really hard to change and replace decades of false, distorted thinking patterns. So it's back to the drawing board. I am sitting down and studying with scriptures, tapes, and books this time instead of just listening to the tapes. I'm taking notes, pondering, praying about what I'm learning. It takes such concentration. I cannot allow certain things to enter my head. I have to recognize them immediately for what they are. This is hard because they are so familiar—it's easy to give in and believe them, like old trusted friends. This is the ultimate responsibility: my own thoughts.

At one particularly low point, I was in the van. Paul was driving us all up the canyon and I began to doubt everything. I was so sad to lose the Spirit and the feeling of love for myself and others, that I began to wonder if it had all been an illusion, that I didn't have a Savior after all. But before I could despair, the thought came to me, *but there's the Book of Mormon testifying of Christ. And I know the Book of Mormon is true. And it testifies over and over and over of Christ.* This was a powerfully comforting and affirming thought and I felt some immediate peace, even in my sorrow. The doubt left. My mind caught hold of a thought, just like Alma the Younger's did, and everything changed.

Daniel went to see *The Testaments* movie in Salt Lake again on TRAX with friends. Excellent.

July 7, 2000
Daniel had a fun date up at Sundance Summer Theater. I am

starting to believe he is doing better. Had a good, long talk the other night. He is thinking more, recognizing wrong thoughts and lies that creep into his mind, and replacing them with truth. It strikes me that we are both working on the same principles and trying to apply them. I see now what it means to search the scriptures for meaning, direction, and application in my own life.

July 8, 2000
Paul and I went to the 6 A.M. temple session. Sitting there, I worried about Daniel more than I should have.

July 9, 2000
Today Daniel played "Never a Better Hero" in another ward accompanying Jake and another friend who sang it for a missionary farewell. He learned it in two days and did fine. He has been depressed and not eating. Jake leaves soon for his mission and Daniel is discouraged. Still no date for Daniel's mission. I fear he is losing hope. He says things like, "I'll never get to go on a mission." He wants so much to go to the temple with Jake when he goes for his endowment, but it is not to be. I'm praying a lot to see things spiritually. Daniel gave us his Primary lesson for family home evening.

July 11, 2000
I'm doing better but still struggle with loving myself as I'm supposed to. I'm trying not to get my high feelings of self-worth from anything but my Heavenly Father. It's so easy to slip back into my old ways and start condemning myself for anything and everything, and again believe that those kinds of thoughts are absolutely true. I guess I have not exercised much faith in my life. It has been too easy. Now I see the need for faith and I'm having to cram for it.

July 12, 2000

My biggest responsibility is my own thoughts. I am working to "awake and arouse my faculties" (mind and heart) to the right and best thoughts which are most like Christ. This is a struggle. I'm finding I have to reprogram the ways I have always thought.

Daniel went to his short bishop appointment (they don't seem to have much to visit about anymore—Daniel has not done anything wrong since that day in April when he confessed).

We went on a walk in the neighborhood and ran into the Thorntons who asked about Daniel's mission. They knew he had received his call. I just said he was going when he is ready. There was an uncomfortable silence, everyone hemmed and hawed. Then I felt bad for the rest of the evening about it. It's a trial. It's embarrassing. It's awful. And Daniel isn't doing so well at the moment. I had to practically force him to eat today. I don't think he's doing or thinking the bad stuff—only depressed and discouraged, which is bad, too, and dangerous enough.

It's really hard for him that his best friend is about to leave on his mission, and Daniel doesn't even have a departure date to focus on. But it's good that he's suffering. It's good that time has to pass. Still, I pray (sometimes) that things could please just speed up a little. I know sufficient time has to pass for the repentance process and that it is necessary and good but I hate to see him so miserable and then I worry he'll revert and do something bad again. He assures me he won't and I do think he's changed and progressed beyond it. Anyway, this is all a temporal focus and I try to not dwell on this part of it, only the spiritual growth part, the hope part, the faith part.

July 13, 2000

This morning in the car I had the feeling that the Lord is mindful of me, that I have indeed been through and am going through a hard time, and that I am cared for and loved. I had been praying for this confirmation, so I was so grateful to get it that tears just fell out of my eyes as I drove. It's such a still, small voice. You have to be listening and searching. You have to be wanting.

Took kids to the pool. The warmth of the sun felt so good, penetrating my skin, kind of like God's love feels.

July 16, 2000

Sunday. It was a hard day for us and Daniel. He got an email from a former acquaintance from his dark times, and I thought the worst, like he had been communicating with this person all along. But he hadn't been. Still, I think he should not have even read it. He gets overconfident. We had a talk and he was difficult and depressed and I got discouraged, too. He doesn't want us to help him or nag him anymore. He is 19.

It seems impossible. We don't have any influence any more. Of course it's normal for Daniel to want to be independent of us. He is so down. He says the scriptures are just words and his prayers are ineffective. This is probably just his discouragement talking and Satan working on him. But what can we expect of a nineteen-year-old boy? Maybe this is the best he can do. All we can do is testify of truth and love him. He is pretty tired of our preaching. He thinks he will learn everything once he gets to the MTC, which maybe is what happens to most every boy. I need to love and accept Daniel right where he is. Maybe overcoming his problems is enough to work on right now.

Oh, how I wish for Daniel the amazing spiritual growth that miraculously happens to these missionaries! Sometimes I am afraid Daniel will totally give in to his discouragement, that his pride and perfectionism will get the better of him, that he'll give up or give in to temptation. Perhaps Satan is working very hard on him because he will be a great missionary with a real and strong testimony. This is such a pocket of time in which he will sink or swim—a dangerous, life-changing few months that will set the pattern of his whole life. We are under tremendous stress. And Jake is leaving on his mission soon. Daniel will make it, or not. This is it.

July 17, 2000
Daniel gave us the first missionary discussion for family home evening. I was impressed with his willingness, his desire, his actual humility. It's a lot to learn and a lot to teach, the basic truths and doctrines of our Church and of the gospel. It was a good exercise and we felt the Spirit. It struck me as such a huge, intimidating challenge for young men to teach the gospel. I share my testimony often with Daniel and he thinks I do it because I think he doesn't have a testimony. I told him I do it because, like the mothers of the stripling warriors, I want him to be able to say that he "did not doubt his mother knew it."

July 19, 2000
Daniel and Jake left on a road trip to Oregon to visit Jake's grandparents. Daniel was so excited to go, I think just for the independence.

Daniel called to say they made it to Oregon. I miss him—even after just one day of being gone. He has such a presence. If he can overcome his problems and take the spiritual route through life he will be a bright light for his Savior.

July 21, 2000
Daniel got home with all kinds of stories. He and Jake laughed and laughed about their six-hour "detour." Actually, they took the wrong freeway.

July 22, 2000
Daniel let me know that our long talks are bugging him. When I bear my testimony, he says it is condescending and annoying, as if I don't think he knows anything. This was a painful revelation to hear but I realize it is true. He shared his feelings with me and, sad as it is, I'm grateful to know how he feels. I got discouraged afterwards but that didn't help. I'm trying not to condemn myself because, hey, it's an awful, terrible, stressful time. He should be gone on his mission and everybody is still in shock.

I remember Elder Maxwell saying that this 18-20 year age is an almost sacred time of testing independence, when kids withdraw from parents and parents step back. The child will return in a few years. I guess since Daniel and I have been so close lately, I forgot about this. I forgot to take into account his desire to be more on his own, at least emotionally. Maybe it's a good sign that Daniel is getting more confident. The scary part is when he gets overconfident. It's especially hard to let go of Daniel after all the troubles we've been through together. He may make mistakes, even more and worse ones, but my work is done. I'm finding it really difficult to get spiritually focused.

July 23, 2000

It was a hard Sunday although it was only in my head that the hard battle was going on. There were many things to rejoice in but I was pretty low. I prayed a lot and tried to carry on as best I could. I made several mistakes but I kept praying. Ward Council was very difficult. The talk of missionaries in the ward was painful. My eyes seeped and seeped like some underwater hot spring. But I felt the Spirit even in my sorrow.

It was Jake's farewell talk in his ward. Daniel and the girls went but Paul and I didn't. I feel bad we didn't go but I just couldn't. All the disappointment and nightmare of our situation has been hitting me as if for the first time. Maybe it's that his cousin Chase, Jake, and other friends of Daniel's are leaving on their missions. Maybe it's how Daniel isn't progressing like I want him to. Maybe it's because I caught him on the Internet reading that email a week ago. He promised it was innocent. He said it popped up out of the blue and he was just going to tell the kid not to write back. But I am filled with doubts and fears. This is his overconfidence again. I'm in agony a lot of the time. I can't tell if Daniel is sinning or repentant. I don't trust him. He scares me. And now I can't even talk to him because he's tired of me.

But dwelling on the problem is a temporal focus. If there's nothing to be done, I have to dwell on getting the Spirit in my life, having faith in Christ, hope for exaltation, and charity toward myself and Daniel.

July 24, 2000

We packed up a picnic and everybody went up the canyon to hike Granite Flats. One part was uphill, rocky, and hot but most was forested, green and shady, We called our destination the

Enchanted Forest, played in the water, ate our lunches. I lay on a sunny log that stretched across the stream and took a sort of nap. Daniel seemed depressed and aloof. He wouldn't eat lunch and crossed the stream and disappeared for a long while. It was worrisome. We tried to give him space and show love, too. I was physically and emotionally exhausted when we got home.*

July 25, 2000

I listened to Daniel today and hardly talked at all. It was better. He shared feelings. I quit trying to teach and just tried to comfort.

On a walk with Paul I stopped and talked with Jane and she helped me. She bore my burden for a little while as we stood there on the sidewalk. She is so comforting. She has always loved Daniel—since he was a little boy. She says he was the smartest child she ever taught in all her years of preschool. She said to have a vision in my mind of what I want for Daniel. Don't go to the negative.

July 28, 2000

The girls and Daniel were up early to hike Mt. Timpanogos with Jake and his little brother. Daniel came home having had a bad time. Evidently he was not fun to be with, grumpy and critical and defensive. He talked about it and wept, sorry for his behavior and fearing he had lost his best friend. I expressed my opinion that it was a stressful time and not to beat himself up so much. It's very difficult to have a best friend who is getting

---

*Much later, Daniel told his mother that on that day he was feeling especially discouraged and went off to be by himself to pray. He was trying to be independent, to work things out by himself, but secretly hoped she would find him praying and be comforted.

everything you wish you could have, to support him and pat him on the back, all the while you are being denied those things. To top it off, your friend lectures you while you are going through humbling and embarrassing consequences for wrong choices you made months ago. No one is cheering you on (except parents and bishop) in this your most difficult, heart-wrenching challenge of your life. It's all hush-hush and tragic and never-ending and uncertain. And Jake is making light of it and telling Daniel to "move on."

I see now this is too much to take. Dr. Matthews said to let Daniel take responsibility for himself and for the consequences of his actions. But perhaps he is suffering too much. Jake is probably tired of being sympathetic and has run out of patience. Daniel is very demanding. I thought it would come to this. It's good that Jake is leaving next week. It will be a new challenge when he's gone. All Daniel's friends are going. I do hope Daniel can go—and soon.

July 29, 2000
I had a terrible nightmare last night, the kind that I've only had maybe five times in my whole life. It was so bad that I woke myself up from tossing and turning and throwing my head back and forth and calling out. Fear gripped me in the neck and shoulders like an electric buzzing. I dreamed I was a bride on a timeless sort of wedding day. It was to take place in a beautiful garden with expansive green lawns and a white gazebo. I wore a beautiful white gown, friends and family had gathered, all the decorations and refreshments were ready. But we only waited and waited. The bridegroom did not come. I began to panic because, come to think of it, I couldn't remember who my

groom was or anything about him. People started asking me his name and where he was and I couldn't answer. I looked around and saw one or two eligible bachelors but, although somewhat willing, they weren't ready. They hadn't asked me to marry them. They weren't sufficient. It was so embarrassing. I was so alone. People didn't ridicule me; they just shrugged and went home. They didn't seem to care much at all. It was me alone who was confused and upset. And it was obvious to me that I alone was responsible for the mix-up. I hadn't done my homework. I wasn't prepared. I didn't even know my groom's name or what he looked like. There was nothing to save me from the awful consequences of my failure.

You think of the poor bride getting jilted at the altar, waiting for a groom that never shows up. Well, it wasn't like that. In my dream, I was waiting for my groom but he was already there, somewhere. All I had to do was point him out and I couldn't. I was the one totally at fault. In a different kind of way, I was the one who did the jilting.

Immediately upon waking up, I knew that the missing bridegroom in my dream, the person I needed so badly to know but didn't, was the Savior. He was there but I couldn't identify him when I needed him most. I hadn't developed a relationship, I hadn't realized my absolute need of him. I didn't know him. How do we know "a master we have not served"?

The evening before this dream I had been listening to a book on tape, *Believing Christ,* by Stephen Robinson, and these words had sunk into my mind, " . . . the Savior, who has infinite assets, proposes a merger with the individual, who has finite liabilities. I use the word 'proposes' by design, for the relationship proposed is often referred to in scripture as a marriage, and it is certainly as intimate and bonding as a marriage. This is why Christ is often called the Bridegroom (e.g., Matt 25:1–13; John 3:29) and why the Church (or Israel) is often referred to as the Bride (e.g., Hosea 2:19; Rev. 21:2; D&C 109:74)."

I had also been thinking that there was something I wasn't doing to become one with Christ because I wasn't feeling the Spirit so much anymore and I need it and miss it. I think what I'm missing is the first commandment. I'm not loving Heavenly Father most and putting him first. I'm putting my disappointments, expectations, challenges and heartaches first. I need to believe Christ can ease these burdens. I need to study and ponder how he thinks, sees, and feels. I need to be like him, do things for the same reasons he did, and then I'll know him and can cry to him when I need him most. Then I'll be the prepared virgin with my lamp full of oil. Then I'll know my Bridegroom's name. I'll be prepared to take his name upon myself. I'll be able to point him out and he will be more than sufficient. He'll be exactly what I need and desire.

Why do I have such negative dreams? Why can't my dreams end happily? But a warning dream is good, the kind that teaches and instructs, lets me know what to do.

Daniel and Jake went to a movie and seem to be friends again.

July 30, 2000
We had a beautiful lesson in Relief Society but I felt we were skirting the issue, not focusing on facts. I made a few brief comments that no one seemed to want to hear. But it was okay.

Everything is a process. I just feel so strongly that we have to get real about this wicked world and prepare and strengthen our families. Knowledge is power. But we want so much to pretend the bad things don't exist.

July 31, 2000
Daniel gave us his Primary lesson for home evening and Jake came over to say good-bye to the girls who are going to camp tomorrow. He looked dazed. He couldn't hardly even play ping-pong. But it was sweet. We have shed a lot of tears lately. It is hard for Daniel to watch his best friend leave on his mission. He wants to go on his own mission so badly.

August 2, 2000
The other day—Saturday—I prayed, as I have been constantly, for insight on exercising my particle of faith. I need to do this so I can move forward and find each day worthwhile, even enjoyable. As I prayed a thought came into my mind. It was about learning to ride a bicycle, which I distinctly remember doing. I was ten (which seems a little old to be just learning to ride a bike). My sister and I both got these amazing three-speed bikes for Christmas. But I didn't have the least idea how to ride one. On Christmas Day we took our bikes out to the street and crashed right into each other. But I kept trying. I worked and worked at it and I finally caught on.

My thoughts went this way: When you want to learn to ride a bike you run alongside, hop on, and pedal like crazy. (At least that's how I learned—I was too big to have my dad running along steadying the bike for me.) You're afraid, but you want to ride a bike so much that you take the leap of faith even though it's scary and you might fall over—in fact it feels like and seems like you *will* fall over. But once you start pedaling, you *don't* fall over. You feel free and begin to move forward and all of a sudden you find you are doing it!

Then I thought of how I've been praying and praying for more faith, to have enough to carry me through this hard time, to buoy me up when I'm discouraged or afraid, to be a little like the Savior. And I realized I've just been running alongside this gospel principle and not taking the leap, not hopping on and pedaling like crazy. It was so clear what has been wrong. I've been giving in to my doubts and fears, imagining the worst, believing the worst, giving up. This is a temptation and a sin I easily fall for. I let it in and it catches me and spirals me down down down. So anyway, I realized my error and made a mental decision to leap on. I just did it. Just started pedaling in my mind. I just gave up my doubts and fears and exercised my small amount of faith. In that moment, I tried it.

Immediately, as I knelt there pondering, I felt the most subtle reassurance, like a blanket light as air settle over me and through me and I knew this was the Spirit confirming to me that I had made a good choice or effort.

That moment was so quiet and still—if I hadn't been quiet and still inside I would have missed it. The word *distill* is a good one to describe it. Immediately after that, I felt peace, the peace in my mind and heart I've been missing for weeks. I was so grateful. It has lasted for three days now. It's such a better way to live. If we have faith, hope and charity, everyday life is so much more enjoyable. Why spoil a single minute? But it takes so much diligence. I know now I cannot let one negative, despairing thought enter my mind. I can't give it any space at all. But it will always sneak in, so I have to concentrate on turning back to Christ.

Once I do the difficult wrenching away from sin—from despair and discouragement, disappointment, selfishness, pride—once I turn away from those things and turn back to Christ and become sufficiently humble and teachable, the steadfastness concept is so simple. Once I do those things I am set free. Oh, how I loved to ride my bike up and down those narrow, hilly, winding asphalt trails in Magnolia Park by the cemetery when I was a girl in California. It felt like flying. In a way, so does this faith. It sets me free from the bonds of this world. I'm so grateful for Jesus Christ, my Savior, who is the vehicle, the means, the only way, the reason, the source and the perfect example.

Daniel had a hard day today. He spent it with the Millers sending Jake off on his mission at the MTC. He held up well until he got home. Then he sobbed on my shoulder all through the evening. He is so disappointed and discouraged about his own mission. The time goes so slowly. But when I get spiritually centered I know it's for the best that he has to wait. If he can make it, he'll be a better person for it. Suffering builds character.

We do need to know, though, if he should go to BYU this coming semester. He's registered but we need to know if we should go forward with tuition and classes. His mission money is just sitting there.

August 4, 2000
Twins' Flute recital. Afterward, we all went for ice cream. On the way home Daniel was rude and hateful. He is depressed and full

of self-loathing. I reacted wrong. What he needs is love. But I think he should know that his behavior is unacceptable. Poor guy. It's so hard not to give up hope along with him. How about a family fast for Daniel?

I told Daniel that I think of him as a modern-day stripling warrior. This thing he has fought against at so young an age is an awful battle. Everything seems to favor Satan's side. The world is clever and busy "laying the foundations of the devil; . . . laying traps and snares to catch the holy ones of God." (Alma 10:17.) This particular type of guerilla warfare with its terrorism and ambush tactics ensnares these young men—bright, handsome, talented, sensitive young men who especially love good, beautiful things and are full of life. In such a wicked world where good things are made to look evil and evil things are made to look good, these boys may be easily wounded, teased, ridiculed, taunted, labeled until they believe what the world is telling them—that they aren't who they were born to be, true sons of Heavenly Father, but someone else instead. The world tells them that they are a select, misunderstood group, that they need each other to feel good about themselves. These are boys who may wonder and worry and gradually be led along through these cunning tactics of Satan until they, in what feels like relief and belonging, end up in homosexuality. This is an ambush, a snare. It's a new battlefield and someone has to tell them to fight. "We do not choose our battlefields, the gods do that for you. But you can plant a standard where a standard never flew." (Nathalia Crane.)

Of course Satan wants to trap for his own these beautiful boys who will make the most attentive husbands and fathers. He wants them enslaved and addicted. He wants them discouraged and vulnerable. He wants them to loathe themselves. He wants them distracted and guilt-ridden, or climbing full on the bandwagon—either way. He wants them to destroy themselves spiritually and physically. He uses the stereotypes and the labels and the media, and twists every good thing to his purpose.

Oh, how I wish I could someday say, like Helaman, "According to the goodness of God, and to our great astonishment . . . there was not one soul of them who did perish, yea, and neither was there one soul among them who had not received many wounds." (Alma 57:25.)

Daniel has been wounded to my horror and sorrow, but he is fighting. He will not perish. This is my modern-day stripling warrior fighting the hardest battle ever, against the cleverest, sneakiest, most wicked, most evil foe, who would have Daniel and all his posterity destroyed.

If only I had known how Satan works! I would have spent my life teaching Daniel differently and loving him just the way he is instead of trying to make him into something that would fit more easily into a stupid, desensitized world. I saw my artistic, enthusiastic son being teased and ridiculed and stereotyped as a nerd and a sissy and a fag. And I let it happen. I should have loved and protected and strengthened him in this ridiculously phony macho world. But I was afraid. I hoped he'd try to fit in better. Now I know there is not only room in this world for men like Daniel, but a pressing need. He will make a great husband, parent, and servant of the Lord. And this, Satan knows. He has fashioned a world that redefines and stagnates and destroys men like Daniel and prevents many good things such men can accomplish. Not very many people understand this. Maybe there is hardly anyone. We are all so taken in. But not in this house.

August 6, 2000

I got really discouraged when Paul told me that the stake president said Daniel would probably have to wait to go on a mission until next year, a year after his last offense, and he should go ahead and go to school. I felt a disappointment so deep it seemed to enter through my chest and sink into my muscles and bones and organs. I stopped preparing dinner and went to the computer where I sat for hours writing a letter to the stake president that I will never send, telling him of all we have learned and how much Daniel has changed. It helped me work things out.

August 14, 2000

I think I learned a little more about submitting to the will of the Lord. It is a hard doctrine, as Elder Maxwell says. But when I turn my life and will over to Heavenly Father, my pride and disappointment wash away. I become humble and teachable. I did this about Daniel having to wait longer to go on his mission and started getting ideas and insights on what to do.

One of the ideas that came to me was something I didn't like at all. But I knew it was good. I think it was Wednesday after my early morning hike that I went into Daniel's room and woke him up and suggested he might like to live on his own, near campus. For a long minute he just lay there blinking and trying to wake up and thinking about what I had said. Then I saw one tear slide down from the corner of his eye. He said that he had been wanting to do that, but didn't think Dad and I would go for the idea. He was so glad. For the next few days he really worked hard and found himself an apartment, bought his books, even set up an interview to get a second job on campus. I never saw him so excited about anything. I know he is still wishing that he'll be able to go on his mission sooner, but he is pressing forward. Me, too.

Part V

Let them not say
We have swallowed him up.

August 14, 2000

All Daniel talks about is how he is moving out and how he is going to be more outgoing and meet people and make lots of new friends. He keeps popping up with thoughts and ideas about plans and opportunities. Maybe this will be the maturing, confidence-building experience he needs.

Sometimes I get hung up on the fact that Daniel lied to get his mission call. Then the call came and he was finally honest and confessed, and then he couldn't go. (He says he didn't really have to lie—he just answered the questions they asked. They never asked him the right ones, the ones about his struggles, so he didn't offer the information.) This was awful. But I think now that maybe he wouldn't have learned anything if it had not been for the dire consequences that followed. If he hadn't gotten his call and then got it taken away, he may not have turned his life around for good, which I am beginning to feel confident that he has done and is doing. I have to give him some credit for telling the truth when it cost him so dearly. And for not giving up, so far.

Oh, I hope Daniel's basic problems are due to immaturity and that he will grow out of them!

August 15, 2000

We went up the canyon and camped with another family, the Youngs. They brought the best chicken, marinated in garlic, lime, and soy sauce and we grilled it and ate ourselves silly. All the teenagers entertained us for hours singing Broadway songs and every other kind of song in an endless repertoire. Daniel was the life of the party. What a love of life and beauty, what a talent for music and memory these kids have. There's got to be a way to use these talents to make a good life and serve Heavenly Father.

August 17, 2000

I went running with my tape player but it ran out of batteries one mile out. So I decided to pray. And I decided to mostly pray in gratefulness. So I prayed for a half hour, thanking Heavenly Father for all my specific blessings. I thought I might be overdoing it, but then I remembered Enos and felt relieved and happy that the heavens have unlimited capacity to hear my prayers. I felt good all day, having emphasized the solutions and not my problems. I try to do that now every time I pray.

August 18, 2000

Big family camp out for Paul's 50th birthday. Didn't get up to Little Mill until seven and it poured rain on us. We ate our dinner in the rain and laughed so hard at what Daniel called "the humanity of it all!" Our cheap paper plates went limp and completely flat on the puddly picnic table. I put plastic garbage bags around the grandkids.

August 20, 2000

I love this description of the Holy Ghost. "The gift of the Holy

Ghost quickens all the intellectual faculties, increases, enlarges, expands and purifies all the natural passions and affections; and adapts them, by the gift of wisdom, to their lawful use. It inspires, develops, cultivates and matures all the fine-toned sympathies, joys, tastes, kindred feelings, and affections of our nature. It inspires virtue, kindness, goodness, tenderness, gentleness and charity. It develops beauty of person, form and features. It tends to health, vigor, animation, and social feeling. It invigorates all the faculties of the physical and intellectual man. It strengthens, and gives tone to the nerves. In short, it is, as it were, marrow to the bone, joy to the heart, light to the eyes, music to the ears, and life to the whole being." *(Key to Science of Theology,* Parley P. Pratt.)

August 22, 2000
Got fabric and batting to tie a quilt for Daniel to take to his new apartment.

August 25, 2000
Got Daniel off to school to live in an apartment. Finished a quilt for him. Lots of hugs. And prayers. Endless prayers. My stomach was in knots the whole evening. This separation from Daniel is a difficult one. We've been so close, talked and cried so much, hoped and prayed and striven together.

I think I'm afraid to let myself feel any joy in my days lately because of the hurt and disappointment and horror and pain I've felt and am afraid still lies ahead. Every joy is dampened and dulled by the deep heaviness in my heart. My only hope and joy is for some future time in the next life. I know there is something very wrong with this way of thinking. Yes, it's best to have ultimate faith and hope for eternal life, but it's right now that I also have to learn to have joy and make each day worthwhile. Or else, when I get there, I won't be practiced in gratitude and joy and humility. In fact, maybe you can't get there without those capacities. I have to give myself over to joy, just as I have given myself over to sorrow and pain. I have to be thankful in all things—joy and pain—to develop a capacity to utilize both to enlarge my understanding and find meaning and know the Savior.

August 26, 2000
Paul and I took off to Cedar City to the Shakespearean Festival. On the way we visited Daniel at his work. He looked very happy about his new life at school. After seeing him I wept and talked with Paul as we drove, succeeding in bringing him down to my low level and temporal focus. It took us hours to feel better. We saw *The Merry Wives of Windsor* which was well done but we didn't seem to enjoy it like we might have. I have no sympathy for the kind of humor that categorizes men with any feminine characteristics as gay. It's all just accepted now that these kinds of men must be attracted to other men. And it feeds on itself. What a shame. Everyone does this. The world is so clever the way it gets us to embrace its wrong, destructive ideas. We shouldn't label or make fun of anyone—those labeled too often begin to believe what they are told about themselves, which things may be false, completely false. It's the power of suggestion. You can't judge people on appearances—isn't that so basic? But we do it, especially to males who don't fit the macho mold.

August 27, 2000
I did much better today with my prayers and thoughts. I didn't

feel any bad feelings toward a boy who gave his farewell mission talk today in sacrament meeting. He used to be a good friend of Daniel's when they were little, and then started being very mean, calling Daniel names and shunning him. Now this boy is going on a glorious mission, and Daniel, who this boy rejected and teased, is not going. I imagine we all leave a trail of hurt and pain along our journey through life. I only wish him well.

Paul gave beautiful blessings to the four of our kids who are beginning the new school year. Daniel came home to get his blessing after his first few days in his new apartment in pretty good spirits.

August 29, 2000
With the kids all in school it was my first quiet day in a long time. It felt so easy and peaceful. I had my Relief Society meeting and then watched Education Week talks on TV. Daniel dropped in and we talked. After he left, I hit bottom. I was not steadfast. I phoned Paul in a panic and he was patient with me. I had a nightmare recently that our house was leaking, like a ship filling with water. I guess I was taking on water from the inside and sinking. I was thinking of every bad thing that could possibly happen (even Daniel falling back into pornography, or acting out homosexually and me someday nursing him as he lies dying of AIDS). I tend to do that. It is a hard time for us and Daniel. He is on his own for the first time. We have to trust in the Lord, come what may.

Plus, the Church is not very encouraging about the possibility of Daniel going on his mission. I think they don't quite know how to handle his situation and have changed their minds. It has been so up and down. I wonder why they are not more open and honest with us. Paul is going to make an appointment with the stake president. What a lot of opportunity for spiritual growth we are getting! There is nowhere to turn but to the Lord. I don't do so well sometimes. Daniel is doing so much better than I am. He is acting quite mature and brave. Last night I had a moment of terrible fear and doubt and darkness and felt, I think, how Daniel has been feeling (which he hides so well). It was devastating—the worthlessness and hopelessness were so painful. And Daniel just keeps going, doing good things, pressing on. He is wonderful. A miracle.

August 30, 2000
I phoned Daniel needing reassuring, and he gave it. He told me he is keeping clear of all the old bad influences and saying his prayers. He is patient with me. Paul is patient with me, too. I remember the stake president said months ago that the three of us had to help each other, that when one or two of us was struggling, the other had to encourage and lift, that we had to be careful that all three of us were never down at the same time. It works.

August 31, 2000
We took Daniel to lunch at the Art Museum Café. He likes his new job at the bookstore. We went to see his new apartment and chatted. He showed me how he put up all the quotes and scriptures on the walls around his top bunk that I printed out on the computer for him. Have we done all we could do? Is Daniel going to make it?

September 1, 2000
We made it to the temple in the morning. I was glad I went, but

spent the rest of the day being tossed to and fro. I dwelt on negatives in my mind and did a lot of despairing. Spiritual darkness fell over me. I didn't pray. I was in agony and must have been unable to change my thinking. I felt worthless and incapable and just lay in bed. I got up once to clean the kitchen. When Paul came home I gave him a bad time.

By some miracle I pulled myself together and we made it to Brother Cox's seminar where I got some questions answered and felt the peace and comfort I've been missing. I didn't earn it, certainly. It was a gift.

Brother Cox was so confident and relaxed, like a window, a transparent window to the gospel of Jesus Christ. There is so much to learn and understand. I raised my hand and asked a question about hope . . . having hope that a struggling child would be all right. I know this is hoping for something temporal, but I wanted to know if it was okay. I know about hope for eternal life but what about hope for the now? Brother Cox didn't really answer me directly except to tell about his own wayward son who took 30 years to come around. But I understood what he was saying.

He was saying not to dwell on temporal hope. Forget it, almost. Dwell on spiritual, eternal truths—who Daniel is, who I am, why we're here, where we can go, how to be an instrument in the Lord's hands to help my son. Don't dwell on how I myself want everything to work out, when and how I want them to. That would be relying on my own understanding. This is about submitting my will to God's. If I can do this, miracles will happen, either in how I cope and grow spiritually, or how Daniel does—now and later. I felt the Spirit, and relaxed and felt peace.

That, in itself, was a miracle, considering my despair. I got centered again and began to pray.

September 2, 2000
I decided to study the scriptures to find evidences that God loves me. I started thinking that maybe somebody just made that up, like it was a "Mormonism" or something. Off the top of my head I couldn't think of any scriptures that unequivocally convinced me of this. So I started in on the topical guide and looked up scriptures about God's love for us. Things were looking up but I still wasn't convinced until I came to this passage in Romans 8:35–39:

"Who can separate us from the love of Christ? Shall tribulation, or distress, or persecution, or famine, or nakedness, or peril, or sword? . . . Nay, in all these things we are more than conquerors through him that loved us. For I am persuaded, that neither death, nor life, nor angels, not principalities, nor powers, nor things present, nor things to come, nor height, nor depth, nor any other creature, shall be able to separate us from the love of God which is in Christ Jesus our Lord."

I felt my soul expand, tears flowed. How could it be any more complete or clear or incontestable? I thanked Heavenly Father for the words I read, for the Spirit testifying that they were true, for Paul the Apostle.

September 5, 2000
Daniel went to see Jake off at the airport. Then I went with him to his Men's Chorus rehearsal.

I had the hardest time making myself go to an appointment we had with the stake president at 8 P.M. I guess it was hard to face him or something. Anyway, I went just to spare Paul having to tell me all about it later, for want of a nobler reason. It was an enlightening 15 minutes. I'm so glad I went. He did the talking. I learned some things I didn't know about Daniel's situation concerning the mission and was greatly comforted. He also gave counsel I am trying to take. First, he outlined Daniel's situation and convinced me that he has a deep understanding. He used the words "unfortunate" and "something like an innocent bystander." He counseled us to go forward as if it never happened and help Daniel succeed right now. Success is the operative word, he said. Spiritual, emotional, social, academic success.

September 6, 2000
The other night the stake president also said that if it were his call, Daniel could go on his mission right now, but he is unfortunately caught in an administrative, generic new rule, which is totally understandable. If he can just hang in there. Success.

September 8, 2000
Morning hike with Laura Young and Marilyn Carter to Salamander Flat. Beautiful, even with a cloudy sky. The leaves are just starting to turn. Bursts of lemon yellow and nectarine orange and apple red hiding behind trees and popping out around corners or dotting mountainsides. The colors were so cheerful and positive.

Elder Scott says that whatever is causing you pain, you should turn it completely over to the Lord. I have to do this moment by moment. I hope it gets easier. I wish I could quit fainting in my heart—I so often feel my heart shrink, these things are so hard to do. I keep falling off the bike instead of pedaling. It's got to get easier.

I am finding that when we give up trying to get our feelings of high self-worth from other people, or expecting to get it there, and instead get it from the spiritual dimension, we begin to love them more.

This is all hard and new. I need to be more patient with myself even in the wake of destruction.

September 12, 2000
Went to hear President Monson talk and Daniel sing in Men's Chorus at a BYU devotional, then we had lunch on campus. Daniel is a little stressed out. It's so hard to have him living away from home so unprotected. He is so sensitive and worries about everything. I pray for him to do some maturing and to remember and realize he is a beloved son of Heavenly Father and doesn't have to be perfect. (The same things I am working on.)

Have I mentioned how I love Alma 32–34? It's the plan of salvation and how to tap into it. I don't think it can be stated more clearly.

September 16, 2000
Daniel met us at Apollo Burger. He is the choir director in his new ward!

I'm trying to say a little prayer every time I have an enticement—a doubt or a fear.

September 21, 2000

Took Daniel to get his last immunization shots for his mission—just in case he gets to go we thought we'd finish up the series. Then to Café Rio for lunch and Food4Less for a few groceries for his empty fridge. He is trying to be so independent. I have to respect that better. I make stupid little comments that aren't right. Why do I do that? He deserves my utmost respect. But it was a great outing. He is so fun to be with.

September 22, 2000

We all went and visited Daniel at Blockbuster. I watched him work. He is so fast and efficient—I think he is worth two employees. What will he do with all his talents and abilities?

September 24, 2000

Sunday. At an early welfare meeting I felt I had to speak up and say, "Are we really helping this family by doing everything for them?" Something else will always come up. What is needed is a radical paradigm shift. I pray this sister will be able to overcome her tremendous challenges, which are mostly inside herself, not caused by external things—which are the things she blames for all her problems. This is always true—for all of us. If we could only change our distorted thought patterns and wrong self-counseling, our actions and lives would change radically. It happened to Daniel. And me.

September 26, 2000

Today I crashed, thinking of the worst-case scenarios. Tried to keep praying. Those negative thoughts seem so real and true. It's so hard not to give in to them. Paul was patient with me. I was not very steadfast but I think I used more reflection in the middle of my despair than in the past. That's progress.

October 2, 2000
I had a little moment over something upsetting in a catalogue. Now there is a magazine for "gay teenagers." Paul and I were disturbed and concerned and wrote an email to them. Now they are targeting children, encouraging this self-destructive and dangerous behavior. When I think of the casualties, my heart breaks. They are calling evil good. The only way to keep from going crazy is to see all things spiritually. Be steadfast. Love anyway. Stand firm.

I don't love the things I used to love. I love unseen things more, the things not of this world. Nothing in this world can be relied upon. There is nothing perfect or worth worshiping here. There is plenty to enjoy, appreciate, and emulate perhaps, but not worship.

I want to do everything I do for one reason—to glorify and please my Heavenly Father, even though everything I do is small and insignificant. He doesn't care about the bigness of my accomplishments, just if I do my best for the right reasons. This is going to be hard to figure out because I haven't been doing this my whole life. I have to change my entire perspective. It makes all the difference in the world to think of my tasks, my family, my church callings, and my talents as stewardship assignments about which I report to Heavenly Father and rely on my Savior. I will still make mistakes but maybe if I'm going about my efforts this new way—out of the love I feel for Heavenly Father with the Savior to carry me through—I will make progress and grow spiritually. Maybe I will find joy instead of anxiety. Maybe I'll find out I don't need to do some things at all. Or that now is not the time.

October 4, 2000
Cleaned house, Relief Society meeting, made muffins. As I worked in the kitchen I listened to Daniel's Men's Chorus CD, the song "Alleluia" over and over. That's the only word in the song: Alleluia. I was wondering exactly what it means so Paul looked it up and told me it's a special sort of word meaning praise, the word for giving glory and gratitude when all other words fail. They just keep singing Alleluia. Softer, louder, softer. The music rises and falls with emotion and worship and praise to God. Tears rolled down my cheeks. It's the most beautiful thing. Why have we not truly rejoiced "because of the great goodness of God in delivering [us] out of the hands of [our] enemies?" (3 Nephi 4: 33.)

Went to see Daniel again at Blockbuster. We only stay a minute when we drop in. He's always so happy to see us and gives us huge hugs. Third Nephi 5:13 is for Daniel. "Behold, I am a disciple of Jesus Christ . . ."

October 5, 2000
The cable guy came so now we can watch conference. Daniel called needing to talk, troubled with this wicked world and ignorant, insensitive people. He is so vulnerable and sensitive. I pray he will learn to love himself even a tiny bit of how Heavenly Father loves him. What can we do but love him? He called later after the Men's Chorus retreat feeling better.

October 6, 2000
For some reason everybody in our family was at each other's throats today. I made great progress on separating people's worth from their performance and not getting my own feelings

of self-worth from what other people do. Daniel came over later and we played Scrabble. Then Daniel and I watched *The Winslow Boy,* an excellent G-rated movie about integrity, principles, and sacrifice. Daniel was feeling bad about himself. I tried to just listen and he popped himself out of it.

October 9, 2000
I made a pretty brunch after the morning session of Conference: papaya boats filled with banana, blueberries, raspberries, and kiwi, toast and honey. Then for dinner we had a lovely salmon salad. Everyone seemed to enjoy Conference. Daniel said he loved the priesthood session and how good it felt to have a clear conscience.

We all went over to Sam and Rachel's and visited while Daniel made some CDs on Sam's computer. He started worrying about how long it was taking. This was a chance to say, yes, we're tired of playing UNO and want to go home now but we love you and nothing you do changes our love. Daniel seemed so relieved that we were being patient. He's ultra-sensitive to anything he might be doing wrong.

October 14, 2000
I wasn't very steadfast earlier in the day. However, later when Daniel came home and vented and was so, so negative, I was able to remain calm and pray in my heart and keep focused.

October 15, 2000
We got our recommends renewed. The bishop gave his okay for Daniel to get a recommend to do baptisms in the temple. We called him and he was excited.

October 16, 2000
Daniel came for dinner and was off to a concert with a date.

October 19, 2000
Twins' birthday. They wrote me a sweet note about gratitude and love and promising to be good teenagers. It was a crazy day, including Enrichment meeting. Daniel showed up and we visited until late. His countenance is so improved. Maybe he is going to be okay.

I learned what the rod of iron is in Lehi's dream. It is the word of God to us—to me. It is personal revelation. The scriptures and words of the living prophets are meaningless unless they touch our hearts and change our lives which only the Holy Ghost can do. We can go through the motions but when something hard happens, such as the mists of darkness or mockery from the great and spacious building, we will let go unless we keep hold on the word's meaning for us personally and our eye on the tree of life which is God's love.

October 20, 2000
We got tickets to the BYU Homecoming Spectacular because the Men's Chorus is singing. Afterwards we took Daniel out to eat where he talked our ears off. He seems to be maturing.

October 29, 2000
How I pray my good, sweet girls will be blessed with good husbands who are free from the awful vices of this world! I pray such men are in the making. I pray they are keeping themselves free of wickedness and addictions. But how can I hope this

when my own son was sucked in? Oh, how I pray for him, that he is keeping his life pure, that those old problems will continue to fade, that he will be healed from the damage done. He is often negative about himself and life, but maybe that is to be expected and is just fallout from dealing with the consequences of his choices. We cannot escape earthly consequences, but they have nothing to do with our eternal salvation if we have truly repented. I think that most of the time Daniel is happy and enjoys life. He just vents all the negative feelings when he comes home. I try to see the long view.

November 1, 2000
Daniel came over in the evening and was so difficult and ornery and depressed. We watched a video he brought for his film class. Paul gave him a blessing. He was so broken down. We reassured him and loved him. Maybe this is the hardest time. The months stretch on. He is in such a difficult stage. He feels he should be gone on his mission, girls don't take him seriously, school is harder than he thought it would be, he says he can't concentrate. He did his laundry and spent the night here at home.

November 2, 2000
I had a nightmare that I was in basic training—the army! Is that how my life feels? Is changing from the inside out the hardest workout there is?

November 4, 2000
Sunday. I practiced patience today, patience with Relief Society and with Daniel. Daniel was negative again. He is hard on himself. He doesn't feel forgiven for his transgressions. I think this will take time. Repentance is a process that takes a lot of faith

and steadfastness in Christ. It may be years before he can complete it. I only pray he will continue in his excellent obedience and faithfulness. This is an indication of true repentance. But you can't tell him that. He has to learn to forgive himself. Our job is to love him a lot. That's all we can do now.

Daniel seems to have entered a new period of challenges and discouragements. It's perfectly understandable and we think he is doing as well as he can. I often think he is doing pretty wonderfully under the circumstances. We had a home evening lesson on sacrifice and a little family testimony meeting. He didn't feel up to contributing and felt bad. But we reassured him it was okay and that we love him just the same. Evidently, he had a bad day at his stake Conference when the speakers chastised everyone about immorality. Daniel said he prayed all through it to feel forgiven, and couldn't feel it. He needs to believe Christ can do what he says he can do. That's what being steadfast in Christ means.

November 12, 2000

Daniel came home and went with us to the stake center to see the President Hinckley fireside. The Spirit confirmed to me many times of the truths I was hearing. But the sweetest sound of all was Daniel's perfect, pure tenor voice in my ear as we sang, "I am a Child of God." I hope I never forget it. President Hinckley was pleading with our youth to be grateful, smart, clean, true, humble, prayerful. He pled with Heavenly Father for their safety.

Shelly is giving us fits. There is so much competition between the twins. Daniel spent a lot of time with her. He says she needs love and attention, a listening ear.

Daniel got his baptism temple recommend. I'm so thankful to Heavenly Father. With all Daniel's noise about discouragement and depression, he is going strong, pressing forward, choosing the right. He was so talkative and happy tonight—full of *joie de vivre*. Paul and I looked at each other and rolled our eyes. This kid is either sky-high or down in the dumps.

November 14, 2000
The cares of the world, small and large, sneak in so easily, without warning. It's difficult to remain steadfast. But, like I said, I am making progress. It is now easy to recognize when I've stepped over to the temporal side. The Spirit departs and I'm overwhelmed by this world. It happened last night—Daniel was here after substituting for somebody at a high school clogging performance. He saw his old love, Megan, with her fiancé, a new one, and fell to feeling sorry for himself and wishing things had turned out differently. I felt so horrible—it was just like the old days of misery and uncertainty. But I realized what was happening and turned to the Lord and was able to let it go. I do not want to go back to that place.

November 16, 2000
I am sometimes afraid I will misinterpret the scriptures. It's really exciting to feel an understanding come to me—but I'm afraid I might be wrong. What a great reliance I must learn to have on the Spirit. I need to have more faith that it will teach me.

How wrong I've been all of my life. What darkness I've been living in. What a long way I have to go—only now there's "light on the subject."

Dad used to say that to me when I was girl. He would walk into the room where I was poring over a book without realizing the room had grown dark. He'd turn on a lamp saying, "How would you like some light on the subject?"

November 17, 2000
"And the country was divided; and there were two kingdoms." (Ether 7:20.) This is what is happening in America. The stalled election is on everybody's mind. It was so close, and the candidate with fewer votes refuses to concede. Lawsuits, recounting dog-eared ballots, corruption, name-calling is the news of the day. It is nothing new. We are a mere drop in the ocean of history. Paul is caught up in it and I am interested but I'm not letting it get to me. I'm trying to put my trust in God, not this poor, wonderful country gone bad. The Book of Mormon is full of the same.

November 25, 2000
Went to a movie with Paul and Daniel called *Unbreakable*. It contained gospel truths. First, everything changes when you know who you really are. Second, there is opposition in all things. Daniel is dealing with guilt. In a talk we had, I felt the Spirit confirm that he is trying his best. Perhaps he'll be all right.

December 1, 2000
Daniel's BYU chorus concert was wonderful as usual. We went for root beer floats afterwards. Daniel was negative as we parted and worried me. I think he's just worried about finals and bugged by roommates. He takes his ward choir job really seriously and says he can't make it to the baby blessing tomorrow. I told him not to worry about it.

Last page. Another journal is used up but I think the past six months mark a great change in my life in the way of much needed spiritual growth. I am so grateful for the progress—however slow—I am making.

December 3, 2000
Our new grandson bawled all through his baby blessing and Sam mercifully cut it short but included the most important things about a testimony of Christ and a life of serving him. Daniel showed up which was a joy to me. I mustn't buy into his negative moods (like he was in last night). He just wants so badly to do the best thing. In choosing between two good things, he agonizes. He doubts himself at the least bit of criticism. I guess this is to be expected after what has happened. He is making wonderful progress.

The six of us went to the First Presidency Fireside at the new Conference Center. Daniel had standby tickets from Men's Chorus. We stood in a line that wound all around Temple Square for over an hour in the chilly wintry dusk. But people were excited and the city was lit with Christmas lights and we enjoyed each other. We got in, amazingly, and were treated to a feast of beauty—the building, the music, the words. President Hinckley quoted the poem "Invictus" which Daniel recently memorized (it was one of my quotes for his wall). But President Hinckley added another verse about the Savior being the ultimate master of our souls and I was so grateful because I've thought the same thing about that poem. It was a big, good, joyful day filled with the best things.

December 18, 2000
It's good to have Daniel home for the holidays although he is

mostly gone, working two jobs, 12–16 hours a day. We went to see him at Blockbuster and he couldn't wait to give me an early Christmas gift—the Tabernacle Choir's latest CD with songs we heard Sunday at the Conference Center. He is so much more wonderful than he thinks he is. The other day he told me how during his really bad times he used to cry out loud when he was driving in the car, just let it all out. He says that now he is still sad, but in a different way. He is so glad to be free of sin but has not yet given it to the Lord so he can't feel his love. I think he is making more progress than he thinks. He is doing right, doing his best, his heart is willing. I pray he will be blessed with an outpouring of the Spirit testifying of God's love for him— one day soon.

Daniel is so serious about his ward choir—we went to hear it Sunday at his stake's choir festival. Also, he delivered copies of the Book of Mormon with their names embossed on them to each of the Primary kids he taught in the summer and gave them their promised pizza party here on Saturday. He really loves them. This is progress. He is on the right path—that is the greatest blessing I could wish for. He told me out of the blue the other day that he was so glad to have gone through the whole semester without doing anything wrong (no internet stuff at all). Thank you, Heavenly Father! Daniel is analyzing his life, learning consequences, making choices, working toward his goal.

When I write all these things I wonder why I am not filled every moment with joy and gratitude. See why I need to record these things? It cements them in my mind and sheds more light and importance and reality on them.

December 19, 2000

This Christmas time is so busy. Yesterday all day my house was in a festive mess of baking and card making and ward fruit baskets. Daniel was negative when he got home. He got a parking ticket and takes it so personally and deeply. At one point he let me know that it was me he wanted to talk to and be comforted by but I was so dead tired. Finally, he made a big deal of standing directly in front of me and announcing in no uncertain terms that he needed some love and attention. We all had to laugh, even Daniel. By then I had eaten and rested and was able to listen and comfort him. Then he rallied.

I think someday he will see that all earthly comforts (and people) will fail at times—and learn that it's best to turn to the Lord. This is my prayer for Daniel. In the meantime I'll do my best to live up to his expectations. Still, I will fail him somehow.

December 20, 2001

I have been on my knees praying about one sister who has such huge bizarre problems. Today I had the impression to be a little tough with her. She is probably hurt and angry. If I have made a mistake I am thankful to know I am still loved and of infinite value. I believe charity or pure love (as far as I am capable of it) is at the core of my actions. I feel I need not doubt myself on this one, though there may be sore consequences.

I need the Spirit so desperately, like a river, to flow continuously through my days, to teach me what I should do and how I should think. I want to be familiar with the Savior's ways. I want to know him and recognize his servants and become one of them. I want to be unashamed and unafraid to bathe his feet with my grateful tears.

January 1, 2001
I read some in my last year's journal today and see how we've had to go through such a long process in our trials with Daniel. It's amazing what I've been taught and hope I am even just a microscopic measurement stronger in my faith in Christ so I can do better in the days to come. It may be such a small improvement that it can't be measured at all by earthly standards. But as I read I saw the process—it's horribly slow but it's there. It's really easy to get discouraged, but instead, I'll get humble and turn to the Lord, remember who I am, pray about Christ's unconditional and infinite love, and press forward, no matter how slow or feeble.

January 2, 2001
Last day of vacation for the girls. Daniel was off work so he wanted to go to a movie. We went to *Cast Away*, the early show. I liked the message of faith and hope. Sometimes all you can do is "keep breathing"—in other words press forward as best you can under the circumstances, hang on, be steadfast, keep striving. Daniel made an appointment on his own with the bishop, but he came home discouraged. It seemed to him that the bishop put him off a few more months in regards to starting the mission process over. It enters my mind that perhaps they don't want him to go at all and are just stalling. Paul doesn't think so. It is taking Daniel (and me) a great deal of patience and faith and turning to the Lord for high feelings of self-worth. Daniel said some scary things that shot the old feelings of fear and dread and darkness into my body. But he may have just been despairing. Anyway, the conversation quickly moved on. We say things, awful things, things we don't mean at all when we are feeling hopeless. That must be what happened. It was a great

opportunity to turn to the Lord and pray for love and strength and hope and faith—not for things in this life, but in the next. This is difficult to do but it's the best way. I've tried the other way and it's misery.

January 3, 2001
Here's a question. If I seek earthly reassurance, have I done wrong? I'm human—I need propping up sometimes. I am not perfect in prayer or feeling the Spirit. I only hope to progress. There is such a short distance between a spiritual perspective and a temporal one—in an instant I go from one to the other and it's a struggle to get back on track. First I have to realize what I've done to lose my spiritual focus which may take me minutes, hours, days, even years; then I have to fight my way back. Sometimes it's easy. And sometimes it's like making my way through a solid brick wall.

January 4, 2001
Daniel was happier today. He is doing everything right. I pray he'll be rewarded with some quiet spiritual reassurance. I pray he won't lose hope, that he'll begin to love himself no matter what happens about the mission. He's so young—how can he deal with all this pressure and disappointment and guilt? How can he possibly endure?

January 5, 2001
This morning Paul and Daniel went early to do baptisms for the dead. This was Daniel's first time to the temple since his repentance process began. He came home all inspired and wrote a five-page story of his experience. I wept as I read it. Paul wept, too. Daniel seems to be growing, he seems to be okay. The story

he wrote is perfect and beautiful and genuine in his 19-year-old voice. It was a great milestone, another step in the right direction.

January 6, 2001
Paul and I took Daniel out to lunch at the Brick Oven. This was the day Megan, his old girlfriend, was getting married and he was really down. He was so glad we came.

January 17, 2001
I love to say my prayers. I'm always glad that after I close a formal prayer on my knees I can just continue talking to Heavenly Father. I can just keep praying as I get dressed, as I go for my run, as I clean the house, as I talk to people, as I climb into bed, as I fall asleep. In every place, all the time. Heavenly Father and Jesus are always there. This feeling is kind of like the feeling Paul and I had when we first got married. We couldn't get over how neat is was never to have to part from each other anymore, not to have to say good-night and go to our separate apartments. I feel that way whenever I get up from my knees now. I need never be alone again. I always have the opportunity to turn to the Lord in prayer, 24 hours a day if I need to. There is always a place in my mind and heart to go to for peace and answers and inspiration and strength. It's becoming easier to find this place and easier to believe it's really there.

Daniel called last night. His big concerns are his school work and jobs and not having enough time to do everything. He wants to be able to please everyone and do every good thing. He needs to learn to say no sometimes. For example, he is filling in at the high school, clogging three nights in a row, after being pressured by his old teacher. He also takes his ward choir calling awfully seriously and thinks a lot about it. His dad and I are glad these are his worries. Daniel is so funny—even though he is all stressed out he makes a joke of it. He has a phony noisy sob he lets loose for dramatic effect. Last night he said, "My life is a living huh-huh-huh!" (That was the funny sob.)

January 28, 2001
Quote of the week, from Daniel: "Mom! Have you read Thessalonians lately? It's amazing!"

January 30, 2001
I read Thessalonians. Children of the day. Breastplate of faith and love. Helmet of hope for salvation. I never knew that hope for eternal life could really work in my daily life. Now, this is where I set my sights and none of my little upsets seem to upset me as much anymore. It really works!

February 6, 2001
I used to say, "Heavenly Father, here is a list of things I definitely wouldn't be able (or is it willing?) to handle. Don't give me those." Then he did give me those. So now I say, "Heavenly Father, whatever is in Thy loving plan for me, I am going to turn to Thee for my strength and support. I know these things may be awful, but I will do my best to endure them by trying to be like the Savior and using his loving grace to get me through and find meaning."

There is no dwelling on the adversity. There is only searching for truth, direction, and guidance, finding joy in the day and comfort through constant prayer. I do not own my trials. I give them up to the Lord and press forward. The only other way is to alternately trust in the arm of the flesh and live in fear. I tried that and it is not the plan of happiness.

The only reason I am grateful for my adversities is because they get me to turn to the Lord. I am not grateful for them because they could be worse or because they aren't as bad as other people's. This is such a minor adjustment in thinking, but has such different results!

February 7, 2001
Daniel did a sweet thing. I got a phone call from him—he was between classes and only had a minute. He said, "Look up Romans 8:38–39. Gotta go!" I knew the scripture and was filled with gratitude. It's the one about how nothing can separate us from the love of God. Such a comforting, empowering truth.

February 12, 2001
Daniel had a bad day. His New Testament teacher was teaching crazy things—that God sometimes hates his children and that unconditional love is a thing Mormons made up. NOT GOOD for Daniel to hear. Plus he was doing a little doubting of himself concerning his passion for musicals. "Is it really okay for guys to like Broadway shows?" he asked me. I get so mad at the stereotyping that goes on in this silly, wicked world. It would have young men believe they are homosexual because they are drawn to art and music. This is a satanic agenda. Then later Daniel called after a Blockbuster employee meeting so upset because of some pressure and a little personal correction he received. Also, some co-workers were berating him because he doesn't watch R-rated movies and they are mad at him because he made a special arrangement with the boss so that he doesn't have to work on

Sundays. They look for what they consider to be weak or sore spots in Daniel to make themselves feel better, I guess.

This is war! A battle is raging in this skewed, upside-down world for the souls of men! How can a sensitive, impressionable boy like Daniel possibly make it through unharmed? I am thankful for the progress he's made and that he comes to us with every problem. Time was, he kept it all inside, all the hurt, and turned to self-destructive things to get temporary relief. He is on the right track now. Sometimes he lets the world get to him, but bounces back quickly.

February 13, 2001
Daniel's BYU chorus concert was gorgeous—the most beautiful, rich sounds. I loved so many of the songs this time, especially the men singing, "Were You There?" (when they crucified my Lord). How can anyone possibly think that a love of glorious music or art is reserved for any certain group that is defined by certain deviant sexual thoughts and behaviors? It makes no sense.

February 16, 2001
Mom asked me about Daniel's mission. But there was nothing to say. Tried hard to keep spiritually centered.

February 24, 2001
Daniel came to our ward's youth "missionary" testimony meeting, the culminating event of a big pretending-to-be-missionaries activity that lasted all weekend. All three girls shared their testimonies. Daniel sitting beside me felt like a blessing. I love it when he is around me. It's reassuring to see him and be with

him. He is doing so much better than last year at this time—a world of difference.

March 1, 2001

It's March already! This month marks a year since we fully learned of Daniel's problems and his last transgression. What a relief and a blessing. I'm so thankful. It's been a year full of learning. I finally began to learn about the Savior in this last year. I'm excited to continue learning the wonderful, freeing truth of God's plan. In the trenches of my mind there is now hope, relief, a safe place to center my thoughts. The gospel is an intricate treasure I can study all my days—like magic it transforms my life if I make the smallest effort.

March 3, 2001

Went to the temple early. When I got home, I had a long list of things to do and began to get impatient and critical of others and things. I went to my room and sat in my chair and made a conscious choice to be steadfast. It worked. The rest of the day was better. The darkness left. I am learning faith, hope and charity. Why is this so hard for me? Oh, well. We went to see Daniel at Blockbuster. He is so open and teachable.

March 5, 2001

I had an experience in the temple Saturday. As we waited in the chapel the thought crossed my mind that the reason I have had such a bad trial with my child was because I asked for some spiritual growth and the Lord gave me this challenge to get my attention. He gave me this awful, horrible trial, he put me through the fire, to teach me about holiness. When this thought came into my mind I felt a warm reassurance.

March 6, 2001

Yesterday Daniel called with questions about how to know if you feel the Spirit. I found a good quotation from Elder Eyring for him. Went to the BYU devotional to hear Daniel's chorus sing. K. Newell Dayley spoke on Christ-centered art. He explained that all arts are really a part of a greater whole, a marvelous manifestation of the light of Christ, a spark of the divine nature. (D&C 88:11–13; D&C 50:2–3,7; Moroni 7:14.) There are those who will use art to get gain or do evil. Art centered in Christ invites the Spirit, builds us up, never tears us down. Satan's counterfeit has no such power. All we do can be centered in Christ. We will feel abundance, peace, and creative energy.

March 7, 2001

Daniel had a little disappointment but I thought it was a good effort. He tried out to be the piano accompanist for the Men's Chorus "Redeemer of Israel" but didn't get it. He wanted to surprise us at the concert. He has a date this weekend he's excited about.

March 13, 2001

Off to Provo for another BYU devotional. The Men's Chorus sang "Kum Bah Yah." Someone's crying, Lord, Come by here. It doesn't matter why a person is crying—pain or sin or weakness or disappointment. The Savior can give all relief. And teach us how to be like him. Elder Ballard says Satan's plan is to get us so distracted and preoccupied that we forget why we're here.

Went to the Men's Chorus concert, which was a pure delight. Daniel had lots of support—friends and the girls he home teaches. He has really progressed socially. This year has been a great blessing.

March 16, 2001
Shopped a little for Daniel's birthday and had a spaghetti dinner—his favorite. The whole family came but Daniel was a little depressed which is understandable. He is 20 now and feels he should be gone on his mission. So we all had patience with him. A girl at his work made him a cake.

March 18, 2001
We got a new bishop! At first I was so sad because of Daniel having to deal with yet another bishop in this hard time. But I changed my focus and prayed for our new bishop instead. Then I was fine. Paul talked with the stake president about Daniel and he said all systems were go, that they had discussed Daniel and it was time to get him off on his mission. We told this to Daniel but he is hesitant to believe it and won't show any excitement. I know this is because it has been so long with so many false hopes. He will get excited as things start moving. He has learned some patience. Paul and I talked into the night about the gospel.

March 21, 2001
Had a sad talk with a sister whose son is struggling with pornography addiction. It broke my heart. I urged her to get him some professional help. I mentioned this to Daniel later and he wept. He said I could tell his story to anyone, any time, any way, if it could possibly help.

April 10, 2001
Daniel dropped in before going to work. I made him breakfast.

He was concerned that a guy was suspended from BYU for homosexual problems. We talked about how in the old days Daniel was sinning but not a sinner, how he was miserable and eager to change and repent. This boy who was suspended was outspoken and unwilling to change his orientation. Daniel is getting a lot of opportunities to stand for the right amid much opposition. He is called intolerant and bigoted when he speaks of true principles. The world is so far gone astray on this subject. No wonder we needed the family proclamation*.

April 11, 2001
I had a dream that everything was crazy and wrong—just little things out of whack. Then I woke up and remembered that in reality there are big things out of whack. It's like being Alice in Wonderland. Sometimes it seems that everywhere I look, things are wrong. In everything I hear there is something wrong. I am letting it get to me today. Mustn't get hooked.

April 13, 2001
We went out to dinner after Daniel's concert. He is so popular with us now and we all love to be with him. What a change. We are excited for school to be out—he is moving home for the summer.

April 15, 2001
We left right after church to go see Daniel sing a solo in his BYU ward sacrament meeting, "I Know That My Redeemer Lives." I thought I saw an angel singing. His countenance was so beautiful to me. I knew he was singing his testimony. He seems so

---

The Family: A Proclamation to the World issued by The Church of Jesus Christ of Latter-day Saints in September 1995.

much happier now—on a continual basis. He is more confident and focused. I'm so grateful to Heavenly Father.

Daniel called a little upset again about the guy who was suspended from BYU for homosexual behavior because the local paper did a slanted 3-part series on it, presenting this boy's arrogant, self-serving viewpoint and ignoring the school's sexual purity honor code and the Church's clear stand. Daniel was so sad and frustrated at the ignorance and confusion of the world. We helped him see that he is only responsible for his own thoughts and feelings. The world has been wrong before and will continue to be wrong about a lot of things. I was grateful that Daniel got it out of his system and moved on. It's so good to face our dragons, fight them, and come off conqueror, if only in our own hearts and minds, which is the best place to start anyway.

Daniel had his follow-up appointment with his counselor at LDS Family Services and called on Saturday to tell me about it. Dr. Matthews was pleased and assured of Daniel's wonderful progress over the last year. He gave him some good guidelines to follow and left him feeling encouraged and full of hope. It's been a long year at times. Once we submitted to what was happening, everyone just dug in and did their best. We did our best to be steadfast, praying, studying, serving, believing, and a miracle happened. Blessings came and blessings continue to come. Our joy is as exquisite as was our pain. I stand all amazed at the love Jesus offers me.

April 19, 2001
Went to a late movie—met Daniel there—called *Brigham City,* a film by Richard Dutcher. We all loved it and wept at the end. It was not what it appeared to be. Only during the very last scene

did I understand what the entire movie was about: One man's painful, spiritual journey. From what I am hearing, most people are just taking it superficially—a murder mystery, a town losing its innocence. But it's about a man turning over his pride to the Savior and accepting his forgiveness for a terrible, terrible error in judgment.

April 22, 2001

We went to the Winter Quarters Temple dedication via satellite. A spiritual feast. So grateful for that most merciful and loving outpouring of the Spirit softening my heart and filling it with comfort and peace. Daniel said, "This was a totally different experience than last year at this time and place." He was referring to the Palmyra Temple dedication, that terrible day when he confessed.

April 30, 2001

The semester is over and Daniel moved home for the summer. We stayed up late watching a movie and then talking. He knows the principles of the gospel and also knows he isn't working very hard to apply them. That realization is a step, at least. Sometimes he just gets negative but I try to turn to the Lord and stay peaceful inside myself. He was so worried about his grade in physical science. He called on the phone and found out it was an A-!

I said to Daniel as he was going off to bed, "We love you so much, Daniel. And if we love you so much, think of how much Heavenly Father loves you—our love times infinity!" He responded from the other room, "I'll do the math while I drift off to sleep."

May 1, 2001
In the temple I was troubled with negative thoughts about Daniel's future, mostly the mission. Will they let him go? But I submitted in my heart to whatever may happen.

May 3, 2001
Daniel had an appointment with the stake president, which was disconcerting just because he didn't seem to remember Daniel's situation. He thought he had left on his mission and come back home! Anyway, Daniel was brave but I began to doubt that he will ever get to go and poor Paul had to listen to my ravings. I had a nightmare that little gray snakes were everywhere and then I remembered I could fly and they couldn't get me.

May 4, 2001
Perhaps this was a custom trial for me—for someone else it wouldn't have worked. But for me it was an answer to a prayer, that I would develop a deep spirituality, a firmness of mind, a strength of faith, all of which I almost completely lacked.

May 7, 2001
I got out all my old journals. I skimmed through some and found my former self so very ignorant and naive and clueless. Will I look back on this present journal at a later time and think the same? I hope so! Otherwise I will not have grown.

May 8, 2001
I lost it. I was getting frustrated that I couldn't do what I wanted to do or do it as fast as I wanted. Then I realized I was separating myself from the Spirit by forcing or pushing my own agenda. I have a lot to learn about humility, listening for guidance,

patience, and submission. This is huge. I finally put aside my will. It felt like a wrenching of metal from metal.

May 10, 2001
The Spirit is so quiet and it takes such attention to notice, to hear, to heed. So many things get in the way, even as I seek it, even as I knock, even as I plead for it to distill on me.

May 12, 2001
I am exhausted. I am too serious. I get so excited about this knowledge I am gaining that I forget to be charitable. Relax. Laugh at yourself. Enjoy the journey, mistakes and all. And don't try to figure everything out in a day! This feels better. I have been pondering and studying and analyzing too much. My prayer today is simply to feel Heavenly Father's love.

May 14, 2001
Daniel and I talked about how we have a need for approval from others and how rejection feels so awfully personal. We talked about how we can learn to allow others their opinions and it has nothing to do with our worth if we disagree. He laid on our bed for a long time.

May 16, 2001
Saw the stake president at the chapel before a funeral. He volunteered the information that Daniel's mission application had been resubmitted (including letters written by Dr. Matthews, the stake president, and Daniel) and as far as he was concerned, Daniel is squared away, mission or no mission. He is right. Daniel is fine. It's a miracle, when you consider where we were a year ago.

I have faith that the Lord is leading me by the hand and nothing I do will be perfect. But if I feel the peace of the Spirit, I can know that Heavenly Father has accepted my offering. It is no good to take comfort (or misery either) in what people say because I am finding out they don't necessarily speak the truth, only their perceptions. Everything in this humanly flawed world is skewed, even if it's just a little—to fit our own agendas. Me included. I so desire a purity of heart. But often my human nature sneaks up on me. I'm glad when the Spirit calls this to my attention so I can get back into the light. It's just amazing how much happier I am than I used to be each minute of the day, generally speaking. It is hard work to do this spiritual house cleaning. But so worth it. I feel free. And nothing has changed except what's going on inside me.

May 19, 2001
Paul and I discussed how sad we used to be—how futile things used to seem and how much joy and peace and love we now experience in our inner lives. We used to think being ready to meet God couldn't possibly be accomplished right now. I testify that it can be done. It doesn't take perfection. It just takes turning your life over to the Lord.

May 20, 2001
I began to worry about what the stake president said and that maybe Daniel's petition to serve his mission will be denied. If that happens, it will be hard but we can do it.

May 27, 2001
Had a long talk with Paul about miracles. I believe in them, but the quiet ones that change my own heart are the most meaningful to me. Outward things seem less and less meaningful. People

can be doing all the outward things right, but inside there is nothing going on.

May 31, 2001
Got a phone call from the stake president and Daniel happened to be home. He has to meet with a General Authority. He has an appointment in Salt Lake City. This threw us all a little and Daniel is discouraged. However, the stake president thinks it's a positive thing. Time to be steadfast in Christ, never wavering whatever happens. We'll be all right. Lots of praying in our hearts.

When I remember to do everything out of love for Heavenly Father as a stewardship assignment, whether I succeed or fail (or never find out which), it is all the same. I am filled with His love for me and all others. How easy it is to lose my way when I fail to build on the foundation of Christ—truth and light, the rock upon which if we build we cannot fall (Helaman 5:12).

I got out my patriarchal blessing and read it. Daniel read his, too, and we shared. I was moved by the promises they contained.

June 3, 2001
Sunday. Enjoyed stake Conference. I think a main message was that we really only have the power to change ourselves, no one else.

June 4, 2001
Tomorrow is a big day for Daniel. He asked his dad for a blessing. I am trying to be humble and submissive. I feel all right. I'm relying on the Lord. For the most part, we all feel calm.

June 13, 2001

I haven't written for over a week. I couldn't. I've been using all my energy trying to be spiritually centered. I guess I fell apart after Daniel's appointment in Salt Lake City. Daniel came away feeling sure he would not be allowed to serve a mission. We still don't know. I've decided that no matter what happens, I will immediately begin to fast and pray for a confirmation of my own, for strength and comfort and ideas on how I can help Daniel. At least I have a plan.

July 16, 2001

Once again, I haven't been writing. We've had a tough month. We waited three weeks to find out that Daniel will not have the opportunity to serve a mission. It has taken all my energy and time to cope and pray and decide how to deal with this. The day he came home from seeing the stake president and told us he couldn't go, the whole family broke down and gathered together, sobbing in a huge heap of sorrow and love. I don't understand why the Church has rejected him, but I do know that the Spirit has confirmed to me over and over and over the truth of Daniel's repentance and pure heart.

Meanwhile, Daniel is an example of faith and steadfastness and humility. He is devastated, but presses forward even in the middle of this ultimate rejection. He immediately got his temple recommend and is anticipating his big day with great excitement and gratitude, all without the customary attention that leaving on a mission would have brought. No glory. No praise. Quite the opposite. Those who don't know him well are pretty tactless. He is getting criticism, skepticism, judgment, and rejection from his peers and others. He will have to put up with this a lot, maybe all his life. At least Daniel showed integrity by confessing his transgression that long year ago. I wouldn't trade that humble honesty for all the praise of men. I wouldn't trade the change Daniel has experienced in this last year for all the missions in the world.

Daniel has arranged everything and we're all set for the temple for this Saturday morning. He is full of anticipation. Today he spent hours drawing scenes for an animated video he was hired by a local publishing company to illustrate. The drawings he did today were of the Last Supper, a group of people around Jesus, a family sitting in sacrament meeting, and family members interacting.

Our theme for family summer reading this year is fantasy. Daniel just finished reading the entire Chronicles of Narnia by C. S. Lewis within a week and proclaimed with great excitement and satisfaction that it was all a type of Christ and the Second Coming. Now we're all motivated to read these books.

Daniel is actually doing better than his dad or me. In a truly manly way, he takes complete responsibility for his choices and their consequences and is moving on admirably, standing for truth and righteousness in this upside-down world. My miracle is Daniel himself. I am continually rejoicing.

July 17, 2001
Daniel woke up this morning and came into the kitchen. The

first words I heard from his mouth were, "I dreamed of the Savior last night." Then my big boy enfolded his little mother in his arms and together we wept.

Thank you, oh, thank you, my loving Heavenly Father. We're going to be all right.

Epilogue

Daniel's therapy with Dr. Matthews consisted of six sessions over a three-month period and one follow-up appointment after a year had passed. Because of his particular prognosis, he was advised against and did not participate in support groups for those struggling with same-sex attraction such as Evergreen. Two weeks after the last journal entry shown, Daniel went to the temple to receive his sacred endowment, an occasion which Daniel described as a glorious spiritual experience.

In the five years following his transgressions, Daniel has remained free of pornography and homosexuality. By relying on knowledge and the grace of Christ, sexual thoughts outside God's laws and guilt for past sins are no longer a part of his life. Daniel stands for truth and righteousness every chance he gets and is often persecuted for sharing his personal conviction that homosexual tendencies can be transcended and in the process draw those who truly repent and are healed closer to God.

He is working toward a Fine Arts degree at Brigham Young University, enjoying a wholesome social life of dating and friends, and is active in The Church of Jesus Christ of Latter-day Saints in every way. Although Daniel has not yet served a full-time mission, he continues to teach the gospel whenever he can. He was recently instrumental in helping bring an English family of five into the LDS Church and was thrilled and grateful to be asked to baptize one of the children.

To his parents and siblings and the few who know his story, the real Daniel is an unsung hero and true man of Christ.

Daniel's mother continues to record feelings and lessons learned as she makes her way in what continues to be an exciting and eventful spiritual journey back home to our Father in Heaven.

Resources for education and help in overcoming pornography addiction/homosexuality:

Celebrating Truth, Faith and Life, www.drthrockmorton.com.

Context Specific Therapy (CSP) for Homosexual Problems, www.theguardrail.com.

"Homosexuality: The Innate-Immutability Argument Finds No Basis in Science," by Dr. A. Dean Byrd, Dr. Shirley Cox, Dr. Jeffrey Robinson. Editorial, Salt Lake Tribune, May 27, 2004.

"Homosexuality: What works and What Doesn't Work," Dr. Jeffrey Robinson, www.theguardrail.com.

"I Do Exist," DVD by The Truth Comes Out Project, www.idoexist.net.

National Association for Research & Therapy of Homosexuality, www.narth.com.

"Pornography's Effects on Adults and Children," Dr.Victor B. Cline, Morality in Media, 475 Riverside Drive, Suite 239, New York, NY 10115.

The Truth Comes Out Alliance, www.truthcomesout.com.

"Willpower Is Not Enough," by Dr. A. Dean Byrd and Dr. Mark D. Chamberlain. Deseret Book, 1995.

Janice Barrett Graham is an award-winning freelance writer for children and adults, author of *Giant Journaling,* and co-author of *Let the Reason Be Love* and *The Plan Revealed* with Merrill Osmond.

Camille G. Turpin has a B.A. from Brigham Young University and has edited for several publishers, including BYU Studies and FARMS. She is currently the managing editor for Tidal Wave Books.